Marriage
[**Talk**]

Marriage
[Talk]

Kim Walter Brown, D.Min.

CREATION
H O U S E
A STRANG COMPANY

MARRIAGE TALK by Dr. Kim W. Brown
Published by Creation House
A Strang Company
600 Rinehart Road
Lake Mary, Florida 32746
www.strangbookgroup.com

Scripture quotations are from the King James Version of the Bible.

Definitions are from *Webster's Dictionary* and *Strong's Exhaustive Concordance of the Bible*, ed. James Strong, Nashville, TN: Thomas Nelson Publishers, 1997.

Design Director: Bill Johnson

Cover design by Amanda Potter

Library of Congress Control Number: 209935575
International Standard Book Number: 978-1-59979-943-8

First Edition

09 10 11 12 13 — 987654321
Printed in the United States of America

To three women who impacted and changed my life: Kathryn, Clarestine, and Valerie.

Contents

Foreword

I AM EXTREMELY EXCITED TO write the foreword for this book because I have much in my spirit to say about the author and the topic. I have observed as Pastor Kim Brown has matured into a voice that demands the attention and respect of the nations. One of the blessings of covering him has been the pleasure of seeing the hand of God upon his life and ministry.

We are in a time of family and marriage crisis, and those who are assigned to assist the masses in reclaiming lost territory and position are being awakened by a call and burden to write. This book is clearly the product of years of ministry and counsel but remains very practical in its approach.

The comprehensive subject matter of this book is vital to our health as a people. Never before has a book on marriage covered so much territory, dealing with such a wholistic approach to marriage, exploring real issues on family and relationships. Pastor Brown has a style that allows him to be in your face while remaining simple and clear, to the point, and effective. I applaud his desire to speak on the areas of marriage and relationships that sometimes are softened and left quietly in the corners of life. He addresses the areas that we are uncomfortable engaging.

In this book you have the gift of years of ministry and the product of a man after God's heart who attempts to live what you will find recorded on each page. Spend any amount of time with him and you will be convinced that the lessons in this book have come through years of matriculation in the university of life.

Why do you need to read this book? Because each of us needs a radical and relevant voice that can center us while convicting us, while teaching us, while encouraging us. Pastor Brown does just that in this book. One moment you will be laughing, the next moment crying, all the while growing and moving forward toward the destiny that God has ordained for you.

As you read this book, allow it to be an instruction manual for life. Apply the principles, absorb the lessons, saturate yourself with its advice and candor. By faith it will allow you to take authority over every aspect of your marriage and relationships. Open your heart and receive what is sure to be a life-changing encounter as you join Pastor Brown "at the clothesline."

Amazed by His grace,

—BISHOP EDDIE L. LONG
SENIOR PASTOR, NEW BIRTH MISSIONARY BAPTIST
CHURCH
ATLANTA, GEORGIA

Preface

M Y FIRST YEAR OF marriage was rough. I was truly a mama's boy and had very warped perspectives about marriage. Add to that the fact that I was very immature and you will conclude that for me to be able to celebrate nineteen years of marriage is miraculous. As I begin to write, I am proud to declare that God has moved tremendously in my life and has blessed me to have an unusual relationship with my wife. I celebrate what God has done for us. He is willing and able to do the same for each and every couple who will allow Him. The journey of healing and growth must begin with transparency and self-awareness. Because of how God has blessed me, I am compelled to share those lessons and the insight that I have received with all those who will read this book. If you will approach this book with open mind and heart, then the transformation that is needed in your life will take place. Those around you will benefit from the new person that will rise out of the journey of self examination that will take place.

This is actually my second writing of this book. The original documentation was lost. I am now aware that God would not allow me to find the first copy because of the perspectives and vantage points from which I had written. The first book was not written to reach the masses but really only the church commu- nity. Although I am a pastor, I have come to recognize that God does not desire for this to be a Bible study on marriage. In fact, as you read, you will find very little Scripture. However, my thoughts have biblical foundation. With purpose, I have written to reach all classes, ethnic groups, and stations in life.

Marriage has become a point of concern for the masses. All across the world, people are deciding daily how to handle marital situations. I present this book to society as a gift from God for all people, so that we all might have the opportunity to move our relationships with our spouses into new levels of success. To God be the glory!

Acknowledgments

WHO WOULD EVER TAKE on an endeavor such as writing a book and not stop first to thank God for revelation, inspiration, and the opportunity to share life with the masses? Thank God for His patience.

Many people were instrumental in the final manifestation of years of talk, counseling, preaching, and teaching. Thanks to my ninth grade English teacher, Ms. Marion Ransom, and our administrative assistants, Rozilia Lyles and Jamie Booker, for being a second and third set of eyes in proofreading and organization.

To my mother-in-law, Clarestine Johnson, the inspiration of a talk on a sunny day in your backyard has produced a tool for the healing of marriages across the world. Thank you for allowing me to drop the "in-law"; you are my mother.

To the best church family anyone could serve, my Mount Lebanon family. Thank you for your patience in allowing me to practice pastoring on you. You give me the opportunity and pleasure to serve while learning and growing.

Children are arrows; they are dangerous when not aimed properly. I have been blessed with sharp arrows that will do great damage to the enemy. James and Kimberly, you make your parents look like we know what we are doing as parents. Jazmyn, I thank God for allowing me to serve as a surrogate father in your life. My expectations are high for you all; aim high, shoot straight, reach far.

Finally, to the lady who turned my head twenty years ago (my wife, Valerie), please know you still turn my head. What a gift you are to me and the world. Accountant, friend, lover, editor, counselor, confidant, teacher, the list can go on and on. I thank God daily for having you in my life. You push me to excel and dream, and for that I am eternally indebted and greatful. I pray that God will continue to allow our relationship to be a beacon for those who observe the Christ in us.

Introduction

ONE OF THE MOST profound encounters in my life and marriage took place while standing in my in-laws' backyard at the clothesline one summer afternoon. As I had done on many afternoons, I stopped at their home to pick up my infant daughter and my three-year-old son. However, this particular day would prove to be anointed by God as the day that would impact my marriage forever. As on so many other days, I found my mother-in-law retrieving the day's laundry from the clothesline. Thinking that I was making small talk, we began to hold a conversation, much like we had done many times before. I am blessed that God has given me great in-laws who have never been in my family's business. You are aware that for many families, in-laws quickly become *out-laws*.

As the conversation continued, it shifted into new territory. Without looking directly at me, my mother-in-law began to share with me how much she respected and cared for me. She never broke her rhythm of hanging the clothes on the line. I can laugh now, but that day, what she began to share with me was not pleasant to receive. She continued to speak about how she knew that God had brought me into the family and how she was excited to see what God would ultimately accomplish through me in the ministry. It was at this moment that the conversation transitioned from future anticipation to the present condition. I will never forget the emotional roller coaster of the next several minutes. Very sensitively, my mother-in-law began to teach, counsel, and convict me into a season of great self-examination. As only a concerned mother could, she reminded me of my God-given responsibility as a husband. Moreover, she very clearly defined the current condition in my relationship with my wife. As if she were torn between two worlds, she shared how she loved me, while she was praying that I would mature quickly and develop into the responsible man that was needed in my home. What she thought was a passing moment became the inspiration for me to allow God to transform me into the head of my household and the husband that my beautiful wife deserved and had prayed for.

As much as I hated to admit it, my mother-in-law was correct. If I did not change in a hurry, my marriage would be over. God had blessed me with a beautiful wife, just as I had prayed for. What I did not realize was that I had never been taught how to be a good husband. Many of my marital role models were not good examples. Most of my close friends were not married, and many of my relatives were already divorced. I was indeed an immature, selfish, ambitious, mama's boy who was quickly losing one of the most precious gifts from God, my family. That day set in motion a great makeover. I vowed to become the man and husband that God required and expected me to be. I was not about to let Satan take away my future and my family in one great sweep. I credit that day with saving my marriage, enlarging my ministerial territory, and focusing me to be used by God. The pages of this book contain many of the life-lessons and revelations birthed that day.

At the end of my conversation with my mother-in-law, I did not know how to feel or express my emotions. I was angry, convicted, embarrassed, depressed, and excited. Perhaps God loved me so much and had such great plans for me that He sent an angel in the flesh that sunny afternoon to prophesy to me.

It worked, I am proud to say. Not long after that encounter, I packed up my wife and son, drove to my mother's house to talk with her, and made a covenant with God. Part of that covenant was to establish the kingdom order of my relationship with my wife and family. Prior to the clothesline talk, my mother and my wife both shared the number one position in my order of relationships. Encouraged by the power of the Holy Spirit and motivated by my desire to please God, I pulled myself together and read Ephesians 5:31 that speaks of leaving your mother and father and becoming one with your wife. Since the day I had gotten married, my mother had worked to negatively impact my relationship with my wife. Growing up as the child of a single parent did not help. I was the true mama's boy. But that night, it was as if I had on a super hero's garment. I was determined to be all that God required. I laid down some ground rules for my relationship with my mother, shared how my wife and children were my kingdom responsibility and priority, and that if my wife was not welcomed in her home, I would not be coming. My mother was forcing me to choose between my wife and her. The Word was forcing me to choose my wife.

Upon the conclusion of my soliloquy, my mother sat quietly for what seemed like an eternity. When she finally spoke, she requested her house keys and my exit from her home. Eventually, God reconciled my relationship with my mother, but more importantly, God honored the fact that I was willing to confront my mother and bring into order my relationship with my wife.

As the pages of this book unfold and find a place in your heart, I pray that it will serve as your clothesline talk. Today, I stand proud of the years that I have been blessed to share with my wife. God has blessed us to raise our children together and to serve in ministry together. Today, my wife serves as the executive pastor of Mount Lebanon, but I often wonder where we would be without that afternoon clothesline talk.

Chapter 1

The Purpose of Marriage

As I travel around the country with my wife conducting marriage conferences, I always ask the believers why God created marriage. The usual answers are typically "procreation" and "fellowship," followed by, "It is not good for man to be alone" (Gen. 2:18). While I agree with the above answers, I believe that God had so much more in mind when marriage was instituted. Genesis 1:27–28 gives us detailed insight into the fact that God had definite plans and objectives for joining men and women together in marriage. Let's look at several concepts that many times we overlook as the God-given purposes of marriage.

Model the Church in Society

Whenever I am sharing with a couple in pre-marital counseling, I teach the man that on his wedding day he actually becomes a pastor. While he might not be the pastor of a large congregation, he becomes the spiritual leader of that household. Deuteronomy 6:4–9 makes it clear that the home is to become a model to the community and a main agent of teaching, just like the church. We are reminded that when God speaks of the love of a husband for his wife, He uses the example of the love of Christ for the church. In Deuteronomy 11:19, we find the command to teach and speak the commands of God to the family, especially the children in the home. When believers are married, God is excited to have little churches located within the fiber of the community. The husband/father in each home must remember that he serves as the model, leader, and responsible follower of Christ. Each family has the responsibility to model the love of God and the call of God upon their lives. God does not hold the husband with a wife and two children any less responsible than the pastor of a five thousand–member congregation.

God desires that our marriages be examples of the church, influencing the communities in which we live. While many communities have multiple churches, the most effective congregations should really be the small family circles ordained by God to bring change in each and every block of every city street. In the Bible, the family was the center of the community. Remember the story of Joseph and Mary walking from the temple with Christ. Be clear that the kingdom family is perhaps the most visible and effective witness that Christianity has today. Sunday morning worship should really be a convocation of smaller congregations coming together for a greater witness. There are several other reasons why God created marriage.

 Marriage is God's way of bringing together two individuals with faith to form a new covenant corporation that will subdue, multiply, and transfer.

Transfer Generational Wealth

The Bible speaks more about wealth and finance than about any other subject. As we know, whenever we begin to talk about money in the Christian community, we lose some of the faithful who believe that money and faith are contrary terms. Proverbs 13:22 tells us, "A good *man* leaveth an inheritance to his children's children: and the wealth of the sinner *is* laid up for the just." A close study of Scripture will help us to see that God created marriage as a way of forming a spiritual corporation that would create and transfer wealth to the next generation. Recall that God gave Israel their land based upon family and marriage. Numbers 33:54 is clear in defining the distribution of land based upon family. Joshua divided the land by clan or tribe when given direction by God. Marriage is God's way of bringing together two individuals with faith to form a new covenant corporation that will subdue, multiply, and transfer.

Approximately one hundred years ago, my great-grandfather made preparations to leave his grandchildren a great inheritance. He, in fact, left a farm to each of his sons, with the provision that the land could never be removed from the family. What a lesson and a legacy. My wife, Valerie, and I have taken this responsibility extremely seriously and have established a family trust. This trust includes plans to leave not just our children but also our grandchildren an inheritance.

One of the most detrimental realities of our society is our lack of discipline in handling finances. Many believers will only leave for the next generation a broken television and an old DVD player. I find it quite amazing to hear saints talk about how much Satan has stolen from them. Truthfully, most of us do not have anything that Satan would desire. Why would Satan work so hard to get our Lincoln or Benz when we do not own them? They really belong to the bank.

As we continue to move deeper into the purpose of marriage, think about the generations that will follow you. Remind yourself that Proverbs 13:22 declares the need for you to leave something for them to build upon. Inheritance and modeling the church are two of the major purposes of marriage, but there are yet other reasons why God establishes the covenant of marriage.

Conquering Our Flesh

You have likely never met my wife, Valerie, so I will tell you about her. She is a lovely lady, a great mother, and my best friend. What is so amazing, however, is how different we are from each other. She likes it hot. I like it cold. She is cognitive and methodical, and I am emotional and high strung. She is a planner, and I am a spontaneous mover. She is disciplined and task-driven, and I am a great procrastinator. She is a reader, and I am a television watcher. She loves to travel, and I prefer to stay at home. She graduated from college as an honor student, and I graduated from college by grace. When we disagree, she wants to talk it out and I want to yell it out. I am a spender, and she is a saver. We are a living testimony that opposites do attract. My point is this: when God joined us together, He knew exactly who and what we are and who and what we are not. In other words, God knew what each of us needed. I have enjoyed some wonderful places around the world, such as Tokyo, Jamaica, Hawaii, the Caribbean, Mexico, and other exotic locations that my wife had to take me to kicking and screaming. I never would have experienced those places if we were the same.

Ecclesiastes 4:9–12 speaks clearly by saying, "Two *are* better than one; because they have a good reward for their labour. For if they fall, the one will lift up his fellow: but woe to him *that is* alone when he falleth; for *he hath* not another to help him up. Again, if two lie together, then they have heat: but how can one be warm *alone*? And if one prevail against him, two shall withstand him; and a threefold cord is not quickly broken." I have found that when God joins two people together, He is accomplishing so much more than just a wedding. God understands that it becomes easier for two believers to work together toward common goals and callings than for individuals to do so. Valerie and I have been able to accomplish marvelous things for the kingdom that we never would have completed without the love and support of each other.

Marriage is God's way of making sure that our character flaws and flesh concerns are brought under subjection. In the very area in which I am weak, my wife is strong. The flaws in my character and personality are the areas in which she excels. Without Valerie, I would be undisciplined and broke. Marriage has connected me with someone who can assist me in acknowledging and addressing my weaknesses in the flesh. As Scripture suggests, when one falls down, the other is there to pick him or her up (Eccles. 4:10).

We have been there for each other during the loss of parents, educational and professional setbacks, and sickness. Yes, God does have a sense of humor, but first and foremost, God is concerned about our spiritual formation and maturity. The Bible clearly states that when God made Eve, he put Adam into a deep sleep. God knew what and whom Adam needed and did not need any assistance from Adam. I often teach singles that if they are searching for the perfect soul mate, they must start by determining what their weaknesses are. God does not connect us with those who have the same issues we have. God is joining two people together who can remind each other by example of their shortcomings and then model the needed changes.

I am writing this book in spite of my lack of discipline because I am joined to a woman who models discipline and reminds me (not naggingly) of my responsibility to the kingdom and body of Christ. Our kingdom spouse does not look and think like we do because he or she has a call to challenge us to deal with our flesh.

Marriage should be one of the instruments used by the Holy Spirit to push us into new levels of service for the kingdom and release fresh opportunities for maturity and spiritual growth. Thank God that opposites do attract. I would hate to be married to me.

Train Future Believers

In the Book of Joshua, chapter 4, we find the story of the crossing of the Jordan River. The most fascinating part of the story to me has always been found in the part where they place the stones in the middle of the Jordan River. Joshua informs the people that in the future their children will see the stones and ask what the stones mean (Josh. 4:6). They were to tell their children that the stones were a memorial established to remind them about the miracle and victory that God had performed.

This biblical account reminds me that God intended for marriage and the family to be a spiritual university where generations are trained (Prov. 22:6). The Bible declares that we are to train up a child in the way he or she should go. I have news for you—we are training our children every day with our actions, words, and lifestyles. It is important to note that the Bible uses the word *train*. I believe that this verse releases a biblical principle. Whatever we train our children to do when they are young, they will return to it when they are old. If we train them to do good, they will return to good. If we train them to do evil, they will return to evil. This is the principle of sowing and reaping.

As the parent in the family, take your children to see where you were reared. Share with them your past victories and allow them to see how you handled the setbacks. They are a part of a great training process. My son was twenty-one years old when he purchased his first home. We have tried very hard to teach him through example and principle how to handle money and what God expects from us in relationship to money.

Our home has always been a place of instruction. We are to train the next generation of men how to treat and respect women. The next generation of women need to be trained how to carry themselves and what to expect from the men in their lives.

Marriage is the university that God has ordained to teach His principles and to model His expectations to the generation following ours. As parents go, usually, the children go. The Gospel of Luke teaches us that after we are taught, we become like our teachers (Luke 6:40).

The church cannot be the only place that teaches the principles of the kingdom. In fact, church should really reinforce the principles that are taught at home. Fathers are the master teachers of the home. If the father has not prepared himself to be the teacher of the Word in his home, then he will gravely affect the spiritual development of those in his family. Many years ago, slaves would inform their children of their history, legacy, and family tree through what is called the oral tradition (verbally telling their history over and over again at family gatherings). If we do not teach our families who they are and whose they are, we will lose our spiritual foundation and fail to fulfill kingdom mandates placed upon each of us. Our children realize who they are because we teach them and model behavior before them that proves our declarations.

Marriage provides the impetus for training a new generation of warriors, intercessors, and kingdom citizens, while reminding them of how far the kingdom has come and what the power of God can accomplish.

Equipping Believers for Ministry

At Mount Lebanon, my wife, Valerie, is the executive pastor; my son, James, works in the family life recreation ministry;

my daughter Kimberly is on the staff of the bookstore; and my daughter Jazmyn is on staff at The Academy. It has not always been that way. For the first seven years of ministry, my wife was the typical first lady. She smiled, wore a great hat, and sat on the second row in the pews. God never intended for the husband or wife to be in ministry without the other. In fact, if you are single and have recognized your God-given call and purpose, you can begin to identify your God-given spouse. Marriage is ordained to bring someone into your life who can assist you in fulfilling your call from God. Whatever God is calling a married person to, his or her partner must have a role. In fact, if we proclaim that God has called us to accomplish a task and we cannot find a role for our spouse's involvement, then we need to reexamine whether the call is of God. Adam never would have gotten thrown out of the garden if he had in fact engaged Eve in the ministry that God had given him. God desires for ministry to be a family business. In the Bible, if your father was a Levite, you were a Levite (Num. 3).

How many times have we witnessed the breakdown of a strong Christian family because either the husband or the wife was active in ministry without the spouse? In our church, we work hard to model and suggest that ministry teams involve both husband and wife. While we are not able to accomplish this across the board, it is a foundation of the ministry in which I lead. Our praise team has husband and wife participants. Our worship ministry has husbands and wives, as do many of the other ministries in our church.

When we first got married, my wife was a believer. But, marriage became an equipping ground for her, and now she joins me in leading the ministry. While she had great gifts, she needed to be equipped and released to use those gifts properly, and marriage provided for that growth. I find it quite amusing when I hear my wife teaching and she mentions theological perspectives that she learned from me.

Have you ever noticed how the world will raise the next generation to take over the family business? That is really a kingdom principle that the world has stolen. Whatever the anointing is on one generation, the next generation usually gets double. I am the son of a minister, and I must admit that ministry came very easy for me because of who my father was. In our church, one of my associate ministers was a great athlete in college. He has three sons who are all playing college football, and one of them is in the National Football League (NFL). Marriage is, indeed, an equipping ground for ministry.

 Marriage is supposed to be a discipling ministry in which believers are equipped and matured for ministry.

Marriage is one of the methods that God uses to ensure that another generation will be properly trained and equipped. We have limited the revelation of Proverbs 22:6 to discipline. I believe that when the Bible speaks of training a child in the way he or she should go, it speaks to much more than simply parenting. Marriage is supposed to be a discipling ministry in which believers are equipped and matured for ministry.

On a recent Saturday morning, we were blessed with a visit from some Jehovah's Witness followers. I was excited to see my sixteen-year-old daughter answer the door and be able to converse with them about ministry, faith, and Christ. That was proof that our home has become a place where believers are being matured in the principles of the kingdom. One of the greatest definitions of a disciple is that he is a learner. We are perpetual learners. We are created that way, and marriage and the family are the vehicles that God desires to use. Just as the church should be an equipping site, remember that our home is a small church with the same mission. A strong and healthy marriage is one that releases the ministry of new believers.

 Ministry is service.

If the kingdom is ever to be fully manifested on earth, we must stop looking at our calls as simply individual responsibilities and ask God to reveal the corporate call on our marriage and family. I am the father in a ministry family. Our children were born to parents in ministry. I am responsible for equipping them to follow in some way the mandate on this family. However, we must not fall into the trap of limiting ministry to the church. Ministry is service. However each of us is called to serve humanity and the kingdom, our marriage releases the anointing to equip our families to continue that service. As you continue to read this book, ask God to reveal how your marriage has been created and established to birth new opportunities for ministry through the life of your spouse and children. God is waiting to give insight and wisdom that will empower your family to become a catalyst of kingdom change.

Chapter 2

The Priority and Permanence of Marriage

What a day my "clothesline talk" has turned out to be. It has gone down in history as a day that I will never forget. It also is the day that forever changed my life and the life of my family. As I mentioned, I was a true mother's boy. From the age of twelve, I was raised by a single mother. The relationship that I had with my mother was indeed rare, precious, and strong. After all, she had been there for me, and we had shared some unusual times in life. Vacations, my first car, home purchases, sickness, graduations, and other rights of passages were shared with my mother. We were extremely close. But I did not understand the pain that my mother had within.

She had a history of broken relationships and had never been blessed to be healed through any counseling process. She was walking around daily with years of compounded emotional pain. Every time any young lady and I got too close for comfort, my mother would, in fact, destroy the relationship. I watched this happen over and over again. Although I was my mother's son, I really filled an emotional void in her life as an adult male. Anyone who threatened that relationship was quickly identified as public enemy number one. After all, I was part family breadwinner, lightbulb changer, grass cutter, handyman, and protector to my mother. I was too valuable to let another woman snatch me away, from her point of view.

Time, however, can really mature you. It was my maturity in the Word that convinced me that the Bible was true. Ephesians 5:31 is clear when it says that a man is to leave his mother and father and cleave, or be joined unto, his wife. This means that after God, our spouses are to be our priority.

Allow me to share a great family story with you. My father-in-law was an old school traditional Baptist trustee, set in his ways and church perspectives. Both of his daughters married preachers. Very seldom if ever did my father-in-law and I agree when discussing church and the kingdom of God. One particular afternoon, our masculinity got the best of us, and our male-driven church conversation became a battle between trustee and pastor, senior statesman and young man. As our voices began to rise, I remember thinking it was not correct to be disrespectful to him in his home. As I stood in his kitchen, voice raised, I declared that I would no longer stay and listen to such corrupted thinking and therefore was leaving. I also made it clear that my family would be leaving with me; this included my wife (his daughter) and my children. I can still hear the concern in his voice when my wife, his daughter, reached for her coat. He cleared his voice and spoke clearly, his words sharp and concise, "I never thought I would see the day that my daughter would stand with another man against her own father." As my wife reached for the door-knob she set the atmosphere for this written dialogue when she replied, "Daddy, Kim is my husband." With that said, we left.

The ride home was quiet until the silence was broken with the voice of my sweetheart blasting me for talking to her father disrespectfully. Did you get it, ladies? Although I was wrong, my wife did not put me out on Front Street. She blasted me in the car on the way home—and not in her father's kitchen. By the time we reached our home, I called my father-in-law to apologize for my tone and words. I will, however, acknowledge that I was proud that my wife had stood with me; we were one. After our relationship with God, no relationship on Earth should be above that of husband and wife. Our spouses should be above career, call, and everything else in life. Our priorities change the moment we say, "I do."

I am willing to run the risk of taking some heat from my womanist sisters as I share this next perspective of making our spouse a priority in life. While I understand why many sisters desire to hold on to their maiden name or even hyphenate their last name as a combination of maiden and married names, can I suggest that there are some implications that demand attention? When a woman is married she receives a new covering, a husband. Prior to marriage she is covered by her father or a designated covering, such as her pastor. This is released to her husband upon accepting the vows of marriage. That is why, in years past, a prospective young husband would ask the father for the hand of his daughter. Although we have forgone the formality of this procedure, the relevance of it is still very real. The taking of the last name of the husband is a symbol that she has received him as a covering. While the taking of the name does not ensure a solid marriage, and not taking his last name is not a statement that the marriage will fail, we can learn something from the concept of taking or not taking the husband's name. Allow me to say, I am not suggesting that a woman who does not take her husband's last name is wrong or that hyphenating her name is not acceptable. Contrary to that thinking, marriage is truly a matter of the heart. What I am suggesting is, it appears that many times in our society women want to be covered by their father and their husband. That is not acceptable according to the Word. Anything with two heads is a monster. The relationship between husband

and wife is the priority relationship in marriage.

Not even children take priority over the husband and wife's relationship. While circumstance can dictate giving priority attention to young people during times of illness and other emergencies, many times couples lose focus and allow the children to actually become more important than each other. When children become the priority of a couple over one another, not only do they circumvent the order of the kingdom, but they prevent the Holy Spirit from operating fully in their relationship. Too many times, husbands and wives have actually grown apart and are not aware of the separation until the children are grown and have moved out of the house. The pressure to remain consistent and focused in our marriage can be gravely affected when we are attempting to balance soccer, PTA, church, and other social functions. Nevertheless, the priority remains the same.

With This Ring

Have you ever noticed a wedding ring? The ring is a symbol of how we should approach marriage. Marriage is supposed to be permanent. I have never seen a wedding ring that was adjustable. No, it is fitted for the finger of the bride and groom. It is not one size fits all. This reminds us that husbands and wives are fitted for each other. In fact, the ring is circular, without a break, displaying the fact that there is to be no end in marriage.

When I first became a pastor, most rings were made of yellow or white gold. New technology and discoveries have allowed us to develop new metals like platinum. The fact that wedding rings are made from precious metal teaches us something else about the priority and permanence of marriage. Gold and platinum do not shine when first removed from the ground; they must be refined. The refining process removes the impurities and causes the metal to shine. When we submit our relationship to be tried by the fire of the Holy Spirit, those things that are not in line with the will of God will be burned away! This will allow the glow of our relationship to become a witness for all to see. Any relationship destined to endure will and must be tested. Although rings do not have to be exchanged for a husband and wife to be married, the rings teach and symbolize the intent of marriage. They remind us that marriage is to be permanent; they remind all who see them that we have made a vow to our spouse.

The Bible uses the term *cleave* to communicate the permanence of marriage. In the original language of the Bible, cleave can mean "glue," much like our modern-day super glue. The bond is tough, strong, and lasting. Let me explain permanence. Whenever someone is gluing something using contact cement, which is one of the strongest types of glue that exists, the glue is applied to both surfaces first. Then the glue is given time to set and become tacky. After the prescribed time, the two surfaces are joined together and become one. This type of bond is almost impossible to break and can handle extreme pressure and conditions.

 Your spouse should never *complete* you, but *compliment* you instead.

Here is my point about cleaving. First, just as the glue is applied to both surfaces, each partner in the relationship must bring the needed conditioning to the prospective marriage relationship. Upon being joined together, they become one. God does not even respond to them as two people any longer. They have become one and are recognized by God as one. At least one other point should be observed. Even though the glue has been applied, it takes time to set up or be ready to be attached. Before we enter into marriage we also need set-up time in which God has matured us, transformed us, and developed us into exactly what our prospective spouse is in need of. Too many people get married without the proper set-up time of counseling and guidance. I often remind people that the set-up time is really the process in which God makes us whole. Many people get married before they have learned to be complete. Your spouse is not your better half but is in fact your better whole. The most disappointed people in marriage are those incomplete individuals who expected their new spouse to make them complete. Your spouse should never *complete* you, but *compliment* you instead.

The Bible declares, "What...God hath joined together, let not man put asunder" (Matt 19:6). Could it be suggesting that when God joins a couple, only God qualifies to release them from the marriage? The Bible is clear about the proper release from marriage. I am asked many times about those who have not been joined by God. One of the areas that has concerned me as a pastoral leader in our society is how easy it is to get married. In every state, it is more difficult to secure a driver's license than a marriage license. No counseling is required, no studying has to take place, and yet we allow people to make decisions that affect the whole of their lives.

Marriage is serious and should be taken seriously. The bar must be raised if our society is to develop a greater morality and value system. If we go to the man or woman of God to be joined, then we should include them in the process of divorce. Society has allowed the legal system to become an agent of release from marriage without any input from the kingdom of God. Maybe we should require counseling before divorce is granted. Maybe clergy should establish more stringent guidelines for joining couples together. We must establish and live by godly standards, ensuring the sanctity of marriage is upheld.

Chapter 3

Marital Expectations

C HANCES ARE THAT IF you are reading this book, the honeymoon season is over. The wedding pictures are up in the attic somewhere with the Christmas lights and the reindeer. Now you know she has bad breath in the morning, and she knows your feet stink and you snore. She ignored these things the first year; now, she's hitting you at two o'clock in the morning, hollering, "Wake up! Turn around! Roll over! I gotta go to work in the morning just like you!"

Anybody feeling me?

Yeah, you remember that first year, when she liked it hot in the house and you would just sweat. Now, it's like, "Can we *please* cool it down in here?" I think I found out that my wife snored in year three. I'm sure she snored the first three, but a brother was just happy somebody wanted him those first three! But now? Snores. I must note that it is an anointed snore. My wife has to have her full ten hours of sleep. If she does not get her full ten hours and a cup of coffee in the morning, it is like an exorcism is required in our house. You've got to go get the cross! If you just say, "Good morning," the reply is likely to be, "I haven't had my coffee yet."

 There is nothing more difficult than having to minister on Sunday morning and you know you're angry with your wife.

These unforeseen issues push you in every aspect of your marriage at times. There is nothing more difficult than having to minister on Sunday morning and you know you're angry with your wife. But you are accountable, so you are afraid to disqualify yourself from ministry. So what do you do? Bring her into the office five minutes before church and tell her, "I just want you to know I'm sorry," because you are scared to go out and minister knowing that you are not in agreement with your spouse. You really don't mean it—not yet, perhaps—and know you are a hypocrite, but you don't want to go out into the presence of God knowing that you are not equipped or anointed for this moment over a silly disagreement.

I have just described many ministry marriages. Much of this is born out of unrealistic expectations about marriage and our marriage partner. Where is the source of learning how to be married? Who was your marriage mentor? Where and how were you trained and prepared for living life together? Come with me as we explore how our marital expectations are shaped and developed.

Who We Learn From

Simply stated, we learned from who we are around and what we observed. Socialization is a great teacher. Our habits, perspectives, and reactions are all formulated through the relationships in our lives. Parents, media, and community are the sociology teachers, and all of us are students learning daily. We would do well to understand the power and potency of each of these aspects and the impact that they have on our lives.

Parents and Marital Expectations

For the first twelve years of my life, I was blessed to grow up in a home where my father was a pastor and my mother worked closely beside him in ministry. On Sunday, we looked just like the family on the fan in the sanctuary. Monday through Saturday, however, was many times quite different. My parents were arguers. I now know that I learned how to handle disagreements in my life by watching my parents. Yelling, screaming, or insulting each other was the normal routine. My mother was especially gifted at humiliating someone with her words. My formative years were shaped in this atmosphere. It is true that we learn first and foremost from parents and family. While mother and father can be great role models, many times what they have taught by their actions in marriage is not acceptable according to the Word of God. Many times parents have put a good front up in the presence of their children. Often individuals with insensitive and broken intimacy in their marriage have learned behavior from their parents. I cannot tell you how many times a man and his wife have sat in my office and declared that although their parents never expressed their love verbally or otherwise, they knew that they were loved by their parents. The problem with that is found in the fact that we pattern ourselves after our parents. Because our parents operated in one way does not make it acceptable. We must take a census of the behavior that we learned and inherited from our parents and family and ask the Holy Spirit to mold and shape us into the disciples that we are ordained to become. Daughters learn from their mothers how and when to display affection. Sons learn from their fathers how to be intimate and expressive about their feelings and desires. The behavior patterns from which we operate as adults are rooted and grounded in the behavior we observed as children.

19

Our marital expectations are many times based upon the influences of parents rather than upon an effort to understand our spouse. Moreover, as parents we must remember that the attitudes and perspectives we display are forming lifelong impressions on our children. We are shaping the expectations of the next generation. Girls marry men like their fathers, and sons find a girl like their mom. Building healthy expectations into our marriage happens when we examine and acknowledge the good, bad, and the ugly of how and whom we learned from.

 The media—television, movies, magazines, and newspapers—all have misinformed us and caused us to expect romance without work, production without sacrifice, and love without challenges.

Expectations and the Media

During the late eighties America was consumed with a television family called the Huxtables. We know this family as Cliff, Claire, Sondra, Denise, Theo, Vanessa, and Rudy. Each week America tuned in to see what new exploits and messages could be gleaned from this family led by a doctor father and an attorney mother. As in decades past with *Leave It to Beaver, I Love Lucy*, and others, the media has had great impact on our perspectives and ideals. Perhaps nothing has impacted American life like the media. The challenge, however, is found in the reality that real life is seldom like television. The Huxtables never had money problems, were always able to fix a situation in thirty minutes (minus commercials), and sat down for dinner every evening. Let's check the record. For those who are reading this book, are you and your wife both professionals? Do your five children all have great respect for you? Can you fix anything that life presents in fewer than thirty minutes? I did not think so! Have you ever noticed how almost every love scene on television begins the same way? The man begins by saying just the right thing and the next thing you know, the two are engaged in a passionate stare that leads to a great night of romance and intimacy. The children never knock on the door in the middle of intimacy. The bill collector never calls after a day of hard work. The children are always doing their home-work or will apologize by the end of the show for not doing it. It is this very Cinderella imagery that has fooled us into having unre-alistic expectations about marriage. I hate to inform you, but we have been led astray, hoodwinked, bamboozled, hornswoggled, and run amok. Life does not work like television, it does not have a script, and it cannot be planned in thirty-minute segments. The media—television, movies, magazines, and newspapers—have all misinformed us and caused us to expect romance without work, production without sacrifice, and love without challenges. What we read and what we watch make great impressions on how we are and what we expect. I constantly have to remind myself that my wife is named Valerie, not June Cleaver, Lucy Ricardo, or Claire Huxtable. Allow the Word of God and the purpose of God to develop our expectations for marriage. We must yield to the Holy Spirit, and examine and correct ourselves. When we do, our marriages will reap great benefits.

Expectations and the Community

Are you aware that where you grew up could have a great impres-sion on what you expect in marriage? Have you ever stopped to think about how the communities in which we socialize impact our marital expectations? Our social, geographical, and reli-gious communities have great influence upon our decisions and perspectives. Let's explore this concept further. Perhaps a young man who was reared in a Pentecostal ministerial environment was to marry a young woman from a Baptist background. Their marital expectations could very easily be quite different. Their concepts of the roles of husbands and wives could be quite different as well. Ideas about submission and how the home should be operated may differ widely. I will never forget how I learned this truth. I was dealing with a couple who came from very different religious backgrounds when this revelation became clear. The husband was from a strict Pentecostal religious background, and the wife was from a very limited church background. As I began to help them with their marital concerns, it became clear that their expectations were totally different. He expected marriage to include family dinners and discussions about church, while she expected little discussion about church at family dinners. To complicate matters, one of them was reared in the country and the other was reared in the city. The community influences in their lives had manifested distinct expectations that each of them brought to the relationship. The expectations were not out of place; they simply did not line up with their expectations of each other.

Whenever a couple is preparing for marriage or is in the process of examining their marriage, they must be aware of how and where their perspectives have been developed. Religious backgrounds, church affiliations, or the lack thereof, all contribute to our thinking and marital expectations and desires.

Denominational influences and geographical backgrounds can play major parts in our expectations. The big city man and the rural woman can find themselves with drastically different concepts of marriage. It becomes imperative that pre-marital counseling engage a healthy dialogue about the affect that community can have on our concepts of life. Community is a shaper of men and women and provides great insight into the personality of our spouse. Community must be understood as a molder of human thinking and development if our marriages are to be productive and Christ-centered.

Chapter 4

Understanding Your Spouse

WHENEVER THE BIBLE SPEAKS of the relationship between a man and a woman, the word *know* is used. The Gospel of Matthew says that Joseph knew not Mary until Jesus was born (Matt. 1). This term, *know*, refers to the intimacy between Mary and Joseph. I believe that intimacy is defined by more than our sexuality, however. Intimacy is the coming together of individuals mentally, physically, and spiritually. To "know" others means to become intensely intimate with them in all areas of their lives.

Sometimes one of the hardest things to accomplish in a marriage is to know one's spouse. It takes time and effort. Only when the two are committed and open will the level of the relationship that God desires between husband and wife be achieved. The Holy Spirit is a great Helper in this area, but the couple must be pushed and motivated by their desire to see their relationship transcend the normal, mundane relationship issues.

When my wife, Valerie, and I started to become serious in our dating, I remember thinking, "I need to meet her mother." I recognized that there was a very good chance that my wife would look like her mother when we were older. I also desired to see my wife's mother's personality and temperament, because this would give me an idea of how the temperament of my wife would develop. I wanted to see with whom I would spend my golden years. Upon seeing my future mother-in-law, I quickly decided that I could handle being married to her. My mother in law is a vibrant, independent senior woman. In fact, she still exercises daily. I did not know that I had stumbled onto a genealogical concept.

Genograms

Over the last seventeen years of ministry, several concepts have assisted me in moving couples to learn and know each other. Perhaps the greatest tool is a book called *Genograms* by Emily Marlin. Have you ever noticed how the Bible records the genealogies of biblical families? The gospels record clearly the bloodline of Jesus Christ through both of his earthly parents. We are products of our ancestry. Years ago the documentary *Roots* received rave reviews and changed the consciousness of our country. This movie traced the lineage and bloodline of an African-American man. *Genograms* does the same thing by diagramming the traits and conditions of a family through the bloodline. A person's genogram might uncover what appear to be coincidences. But these patterns of relationships and behavior are not coincidental; they are the result of learning family scripts.[1] Charting a family genogram can assist in recognizing family traits for many things, such as the tendency to divorce, health concerns, substance issues, sexual sins, mental diseases, generational curses, and other family characteristics.[2] In addition, a genogram can trace concerns based upon age and gender when detailed information is gathered and examined. A genogram becomes a vital component in allowing couples to communicate concerns and become knowledgeable about the past of each other. It makes us aware of the prospective concerns and prepares us to understand the behavior of our perspective spouse. In short, a genogram allows us to know one another.[3]

A basic genogram can be developed by listing the paternal and maternal parents, grandparents, and great-grandparents and recording under each name characteristics such as age of death, personality, shortcomings, marital status, and any other valuable characteristics and traits.[4]

Until we have formally tracked and examined our bloodline, hidden strongholds can go unnoticed and unrecognized. A spirit unrecognized can cause great detriment before it is properly identified and dealt with spiritually. Therefore, by exploring the generational development of a couple, we are equipped to become proactive rather than reactive in handling relational concerns. If, for instance, after tracking and charting a family's genogram, it is recognized that infidelity is a concern, we can adjust our behavior, relationships, and environment to reduce the possibility of developing undesired relationships. For years, the Christian community has been informed and taught about generational curses and strongholds, but the use of a genogram brings to life in a very tangible way the evidence to partner with the pragmatic instruction.

It is not enough to know the Bible; we must be doers of the Word. Genograms enable us to be doers and apply the spiritual authority of God when confronting personal and corporate issues in our marriages. When couples come together and develop a three-generation diagram (grandparents, parents, themselves), lights come on that have previously not been seen. This new illumination of information becomes a map helping a couple to address, pray for, and break strongholds that have existed for years. A genogram does not have to be complicated to be effective. A simple genogram can unlock a vast amount of information.

How We Are Wired

I am sure that by now you are aware that men and women think very differently. While we may be aware of our differences, I have found that we are not educated on our differences. Women must be committed to learning how to speak and communicate in a language men understand. Men as well must become students of women and communicate on their frequency. This can only be accomplished when we begin to study and understand the communication process of men and women.

I will never forget how I learned this truth. The women in our church were having a prayer breakfast many years ago. Upon the completion of the prayer breakfast, I found out that some of the women had displayed behavior toward each other that, shall we say, was not favorable for Christian sisters. In fact, several women were upset because of who was allowed to be the leader of the moment and the manner in which she had planned and led the ministry moment. They had disagreements over simple things like cooking the eggs for the breakfast. I remember becoming very discouraged over the trivial things the ladies were upset about. As I developed in ministry, I came to understand and expect the women to have their differences whenever there was a female-only ministry moment. It was how they had been wired at creation that caused the problems.

Without running the risk of sounding insensitive and being accused of being a sexist, let me share a perspective about men. Have you ever noticed how men cannot even play a basketball game without an argument over a foul or the score? We have a gymnasium at our church. I am always amazed at how the same Spirit-filled guys, who on Sunday morning were praising God together, cannot play a basketball game, Ping-Pong, or shoot pool without challenging the masculinity of each other. All of this is because of how we were wired at creation.

According to Genesis 1:28, Adam was called to subdue and have authority. In Genesis 3:15, God tells the woman that she will have enmity between her seed and the seed of the enemy. These two Scripture passages give great insight on how men and women are wired. Men are "warriors" by nature, and women are "warring" by nature.

The reason men cannot play a simple game of basketball without arguing is because they are warriors. A warrior must battle and must win. A warrior is always looking for a fight and an enemy. Let me hesitate to share here that a man without an enemy is dangerous. Men will find an enemy. Men who are abusive to their wives are usually men who have never been shown the proper enemy and therefore make their wives the enemy. A man without a designated enemy is a man consumed with anger. Each man is wired and created for a battle. The kingdom has many times failed to show men the real enemy. One of the main reasons why our young men are gang-banging is that the church has not trained them to identify the correct enemy—sin.

Remember that Adam had been in the garden before Eve. Theologically, we know that the serpent was in the garden before Adam. Yet when the transaction happens, Adam blames the woman. Later, however, Eve identifies the serpent as the deceiver that has tricked them into transgression. Adam, I believe, was not able to see the serpent in the garden but was called to dominate him. While men are warriors by nature, they do not have the ability to see the enemy. Women, however, have been wired to see the enemy but are not called to be warriors. In fact, when a women sees the enemy, something inside of her snaps. God has wired a woman to have hatred for the enemy. A man can work next to a mass murderer every day and never discern that spirit. A woman can meet someone for the first time and immediately discern that something about that person is wrong. Men are warriors. Women are warring.

Many times, I am fooled by the young people my children bring home. I am easy to fool, but my wife is never fooled. She has been blessed and wired by God to see the enemy. Men must understand that women can see the enemy when we cannot. Statistics prove that most women know when their husband has had an affair before he confesses. This spiritual eye that a woman has is her gift from God for the man. Remember, the Bible says that it is not good for man to be alone. The Bible never declares that it is not good for a woman to be alone. Further, the Bible reveals that he that "findeth a wife findeth a good thing," not she that findeth a husband (Prov. 18:22).

Women are made to see the enemy, get mad about his presence, and point the enemy out to her husband. Upon receiving the revelation of the presence of the enemy, the husband is to wage war and destroy the presence. When a husband partners his warrior spirit with the warring spirit of a woman, they become a powerful team, armed and dangerous, ready to wage a victorious war against Satan. Here are several other attributes of men and women that will help to develop our understanding of the differences between husbands and wives. Men are warriors, competitive, vision-driven, and linear thinkers who process their thoughts in a cave. Men usually make decisions based upon a vision. A family will find it difficult to live with any man without a vision for himself and his family. Women must understand that men typically make decisions based upon a linear movement of existence. A woman does not forget and let things go as easily as a man does. Since men process linearly, they do not always reflect on what was done the last time and measure their decisions by past experiences. While this can be a great help in moving forward it can also create an environment that prohibits learning from past mistakes. Finally, men process in a cave, a place of solitude and thinking. Ladies, how many times have you discussed something with your husbands and expected a response as soon as you finished sharing, only to feel ignored? But several days later, your husband returns with a response to your suggestion or question, only to find you angry and unresponsive. Men will gather the facts, go into the cave by themselves, and think through the dynamics and make the decisions down inside that cave.

Women are ideal-driven. They are circular in thought, on-the-spot processors, and detail-driven. Just as a woman's body works on a monthly cycle, we must understand that her processing and decision making does as well. Women can usually forgive but have a harder time forgetting than a man because past experiences are processed circularly, while men tend to process linearly. While past experiences move beyond our horizon of reflection when we process circularly, they are easily reintroduced psychologically through present experiences that become emotion triggers. While men process in a cave, women process on the spot. They typically are quick decision-makers, while men are not. Have you ever noticed that most women will go into a store and shop for clothing by browsing, while most men already know what they are looking for when they enter the store? A woman will touch every rack and every dress, and when approached by a salesperson will say, "I'm just looking." When men go to the store, it is to buy a blue shirt or something that has already been determined. Men typically do not browse; they walk into the store, find a sales clerk, and ask where the blue shirts are. If informed that no blue shirts are available, the man usually leaves. Women will tell you they do not know what they are looking for, but they will know it when they see it.

People are wired differently. Women can remember the color of the socks a man at church had on, while the average man will not even remember that the man was in church. When we begin to understand how we are wired, we become open to understanding why God has called men and women to become one. We compliment each other. When a man finds his Eve, a missing piece of him is returned. The rib that she was created from makes him complete once again. A man will not really feel complete until he finds his Eve. She is the missing rib in his side. The very differences that many times cause us to have marital complications are also the greatest gift to couples.

We are not the same. We do not think alike. We are wired differently because we have different calls. The man and woman who have come to know and appreciate their differences are ready to accomplish great things for the kingdom of God. Our greatest attributes are the missing links that unlock the potential of our spouses. We must learn to study our spouses so that we might have the pleasure of knowing them and the excitement of sharing this journey of life with them.

Chapter 5

How Men Are Wired

THE BIBLE SAYS IN Genesis 2:18 that it is not good that man should be alone. It is amazing to discover, however, that the Bible never declares this about woman, only man. Discovering how God wired men and women will revolutionize how we respond to each other in marital relationships. If men can identify the reasons why they act and think as they do, they can better understand how to train their actions in relationship to their wives. As well, when women begin to understand why men respond to certain situations based upon their psychological fingerprints, women will be able to satisfy the will of God for their lives by truly becoming helpmeets fashioned after God's heart. While there are exceptions to all rules, we will take time to explore the wiring of men over the next several pages.

Linear Thinkers

How many times have you heard of this scenario in a marriage: the couple has a disagreement, and upon reconciling their differences and making up, the husband is ready to be intimate—only to recognize that his wife has not moved into a mentality that will allow her to be affectionate? No, it is not because men have a one-track mind but because men usually think linearly. Once a man has dealt with something, it is deleted from his memory much easier because he thinks on a straight line. Yesterday, last week, and even moments ago are things of the past. We will discuss later how women think with a circular pattern of processing. This can sometimes cause problems in the marriage because it can appear as if men move on too easily and women are slow to forgive and forget. Because God desired for us to be different, men must always be aware that women are going to take more time to work through their feelings and emotions, while men can usually delete circumstances and move to the next mental destination faster. I often remind men that women can remember much more about previous conversations and situations because they think differently than men.

Cave Men

Another aspect of how men process and think is what I call the "caveman mentality." Before you kill me, hear me out. I am not talking about how men treat their wives, but how men think and mentally process the events of life. For example, a man's wife will come in and desire to make a decision on daycare for the child. She has done research and has made an informed decision matrix. She sits down with her husband and desires to make an educated and informed decision. The problem is that she wants to make the decisions right at that moment. She has planned and knows it is decision time. Men do not make decisions that way. A man usually will revert into the "cave" for solitude and meditation. Many times the wife is upset because it appears as if the man is not serious or does not take the decision seriously. In actuality, he is thinking in his cave. Several days later, the man will exit his cave and declare he has thought about what his wife shared and is ready to make a decision about daycare. Unless the wife recognizes how men make decisions, she will find herself upset over his perceived lack of support about the decision in the first place.

Men need time and space to make decisions. They feel intimidated when asked to make major decisions on the spot. Give a man time and he will prove his sensitivity and concern with a decision that has been processed over and over many times. This is often the case in my home with major decisions. Women tend to call men procrastinators. While men can tend to put things off, many times it is simply the process that God has equipped men with and not their lack of commitment to action. I usually visit a car dealer several times to test drive a car before I purchase it. Women can usually drive onto the dealership property and feel comfortable purchasing a car the first time they see it. Men very rarely join a ministry the first time they come; however, women will connect with the fellowship and make that decision before their first worship experience is even finished.

Lions: Must Be Free to Roam

I cannot begin to tell you how many nights I have been sitting at home watching television or reading a book and just needed to go for a ride. As I get up and put on my shoes, my wife would ask, "Where are you going?" "I don't know," usually would be my reply. Men have a need for freedom. When sharing with new brides, I often remind them that men have a lion inside of them that needs to roam once in a while.

Women are nurturers by comparison and like having everyone around. Men, on the other hand, need space. It can prove to be detrimental to any relationship to smother a man. A trip to the store can be some of the most beneficial time a woman can allow a man to have. A one-hour road trip to the car wash can be therapeutic in multiple ways. In fact, have you ever noticed that a caged lion has a bad attitude in the movies? Men are restricted all day on the job and need to have a moment of freedom to combat the feelings and pressures of life. It is often said that women are much tougher than men. I agree. Women multitask extremely well. Most men do not. An acknowledged time for allowing the lion to roam is one of the greatest gifts a woman can give to a man. Suggest a trip over to his brother's house, a grocery store run, or a trip to the basketball court, and watch the power of God release a new level in you relationship.

Small-Picture Vision

Another mental peculiarity about men is to be found in the fact that men rarely see the larger picture. Have you ever observed men shopping? A man will go into the mall, look at the directory, and find the store that sells men's clothing. He will then go to that particular store, walk in, go directly to the shirt section, secure the blue shirt he came for, and walk directly toward the cashier. He does not usually spend time looking at suits, shoes, or slacks, unless they were on his list in the first place. Twenty minutes later, the man exits the store with one bag containing his newly purchased blue shirt. This simply points to the fact that men are usually small-picture people. Because of this, men generally do not multi-task very well. Contrary to women, men are proficient at handling one thing at a time. For instance, if a man starts building the fence for the back yard, distractions must be limited. A man will become upset when called to the phone or asked to stop for a moment to eat lunch. This is also why men, the procrastinators that they may be, do not like to stop a project once it is started. They want to finish it without interruption, all at once.

Greater proof of this can be found in observing how the family takes trips, especially when the family car is used as the mode of transportation for the family vacation. Dad gets in the driver's seat, already upset because the family is leaving later than originally scheduled. After riding for two hours, tension builds in the vehicle because no one wants to acknowledge that they need to stop for a restroom break. The man usually wants to keep driving because he is wired to see the small picture, the beginning and the end.

Not only do men usually see the small picture, but they also see things in black and white. Wives are there to add the color, the details, if you will. Men will plan the vacation trip but not remember to pack any drinks and snacks, make hotel reservations, or develop a vacation itinerary.

Visual

Have you ever noticed that men usually have more addictions to pornography than women? That is because men are visual. Men are aroused and stimulated through visual stimuli, while women are conceptual. We will explain this more in the chapter about how women are wired.

I cannot tell you how often I have been in a counseling session and the subject of dress and garments has come up. Women, especially Christian women, tend to be offended by requests from their husband to dress up in pumps and short garments as a means of stimulating their husband for intimacy. Please know that the average husband does not care that his wife is a size 14, 16, or 18; he is visual. Men like seeing their wives dress in colors, heels, and other types of clothing that appeal to their visual expectations. While many times women are very self-conscious, men love "seeing" their wives and become excited to know that she was willing to dress for his visual approval.

Chapter 6

The Role of the Kingdom Husband

S OMETIMES WE ARE SO complicated that we miss simple revelations. The word *husband* is the adjective that God used to describe the role of the man in marriage. What is a husband? According to the dictionary, the word *husband* comes from the words *house* and *band*. These two words give great insight into the role of the husband. First, it is clear that the man is called to the home (house). Perhaps that is why God defines the ministry in the home as the first priority for those who will lead in the temple. It is easy to see the erosion of our community in relationship to the absence of male leadership in the home. Although I was raised without a man in our home as a teenager, there were still men in my church and community who provided male direction and role modeling.

 The man is vital to establishing the set order of the family. If the head is out of order, the arms, legs, hands, and everything else are out of order.

The husband is called to minister first in his home. Secondly, he is called to be a band. The man is to be the safety and strength, the band around the family. It can be said that the band should set the limits, structures, and parameters for the movement of the family. A band is tight but flexible, strong but stretchable, like a rubber band, for example. The man keeps it together. As the band of the family, he is called to make sure that needs are met and standards are set. My children know the limits of our family. They have been made aware of the standards by which we live. The parameters for living in our home are clearly defined and established for everyone. The man is vital to establishing the set order of the family. If the head is out of order, the arms, legs, hands, and everything else are out of order. Finally, a band must be able to handle the pressure of stretching without breaking or snapping. As my grandfather used to say, "Pressure will burst a pipe." However, the man must be able to handle the pressures of life and sustain a healthy strength and endurance. The "house-band" is the first line of defense for the family. In order to impact the family he is impacted first. I often tell people, in order to get to my family you must come through me. I am the band that surrounds my wife, children, and our potential. Perhaps that is why men must be warriors. Stand up, "house-band," and fight for the future of your family.

Another definition of a husband is that he is a manager or steward. I can remember years ago when my wife ministered at a local church. The church was not a small church and had the ability to share resources. After spending a full day sharing with their financial leadership, they gave my wife a box of chocolates. As her manager, I felt it was my responsibility to share with the pastor my concern over how my wife was valued. I am her husband (manager). As her husband, it became my responsibility to make sure that no one took advantage of her. It was not about money; it was about respect for who she is in the body of Christ. In the past, I have met with her college professors and other individuals that I thought were disrespecting her. Husbands must remember that they are the steward and manager of the family. God has given you a great gift, but you have an even greater responsibility to manage and grow those who live in your home.

The final definition of a husband is that he is an agricultural being. According to the dictionary, a husbandman is a farmer. What do farmers do? They grow plants, food, and maintain agriculture. As a husband, I am a farmer. What do I grow? I grow Valerie's, James's, Kimberly's, and Jazmyn's lives. I am anointed to grow the people in my family, especially my wife. The Bible declares that we are to be husbands to one wife (1 Tim. 3:12). This is more than a station in life relative to marriage and service in the kingdom. It is also about the role and relationship of a husband to his wife. "One wife" means simply that I am not anointed to grow anyone else but Valerie. There are things that are particular about my wife that God has equipped me to understand and develop. Any man who is married and cannot see the growth and development of his wife has dropped the ball in the responsibility of being a husband. A man in the role of husband must understand that he is a cultivator, a planter, a pruner, and the gardener in the life of his wife. The wife should be the greatest masterpiece for a husband. When people see my wife, they should see how great her husband is by how she is growing and maturing in the faith. I must remind all men that farming is time-consuming and driven by faith. The farmer who does not spend time working the relationship of his crop will yield a weak harvest. This can be said as well for the husband who does not invest time in his wife. A great harvest of growth will require a great investment of time. Turn off the television, educate your wife on her weaknesses with compassion, celebrate her growth with excitement, and observe as God rewards the time and investment. Proverbs 31 says that her husband will be well known and respected in the gates of the city. Perhaps

41

this is because they will recognize the growth in the woman as a byproduct of her relationship with her husband, the farmer.

I can still remember the pride and joy of my uncle in Gumberry, North Carolina, as he would ride out every Sunday after church. He would ride through the country to observe his peanut fields. His chest would swell up and his eyes would gleam because the farmer in him was proud to see those green plants spreading out across acres of fields and transforming the barren soil into opportunities of great harvest. That is the joy of being a husband: watching your wife grow, mature, and develop, while knowing that you have been instrumental in the process.

Headship

One of the most misunderstood concepts in the body of Christ is headship. Whenever I am sharing with a couple preparing to be married, I feel compelled by the Spirit to spend time talking about the area of headship. Men always like to point out to the women that God called them to be the head of the household. As proud as I am to be a man, many days I spend time asking God if He was sure that men were called to be the head. I can just think of a better order for the family. But true to the Word of God, the responsibility of leading the family is given to the man. But what does it really mean to be the head of the family?

 God is not concerned about the size of the congregation but the spiritual health of the people.

Much has been written and said about the man being the head of the household. The Bible is clear that God ordained man to be the head of the household. But headship is more than a title. The day a man is joined with his wife in matrimony, he actually becomes a pastor. He becomes the spiritual leader and role model to his wife and the children. I have been blessed to pastor thousands in church, but the call is no less for the husband who pastors only his family. Just as God holds me accountable for the spiritual direction of Mount Lebanon Church, God will hold the husband accountable for the family. At our church, I am the chief teacher and minister. In the home, the man is the chief teacher and minister. Please understand that many times the man might not feel comfortable teaching the family but knows that God does hold him accountable for the family being taught. Just as I cover the believers in the church I serve, the husband is to cover the family spiritually, physically, and emotionally. While they may never refer to a man as "reverend," God has expectations that the spiritual flavor and tone for the family be established and led by the man.

Covering

We mentioned earlier the need for the husband to cover the family. Covering is not always understood as clearly as it should be. Do you remember the old western television show *Gunsmoke*? In the show, many times Matt Dillon would ask Festus, his deputy, to cover him during a gunfight. Festus would then make himself more visible and shoot at the enemy to distract the enemy from seeing the movement of marshal Matt Dillon. Therein lies the foundation for the theory of covering. When you cover someone, you make yourself a visible target to take the attacks that could destroy someone else. In short, you allow yourself to be shot at instead of someone else. You become a target so that someone else can move freely without danger. The husband is the covering of the family. He makes himself the target to protect the family spiritually. This means that Satan will potentially come after the husband with a different level of attack. Satan knows that if he can get the husband, then the family is vulnerable. That is why men must fellowship and remain spiritually focused. We are targets of the adversary.

Responsibility

When you study the events surrounding Adam and Eve in the garden, we can learn some profound things about the role of the husband and wife. First, notice that when Eve eats from the fruit, she and Adam are not evicted from the garden. In fact, God does not even show up. The moment that Adam eats of the fruit, God shows up asking questions like, "Adam where are you?" (Gen. 3:17). As unfair as it seems, God appears to hold Adam to a different standard because, I believe, Adam (the man) holds the reigns of responsibility for the spiritual movement and development of the family. God never gets upset with Eve because she is not the responsible party. I often tell the men at our church that "being a man is not easy, but someone has to do it." Listen to me! God did not choose Adam because he was smarter or stronger. God simply desires order. If no one is acknowledged as the leader, then God has no one to hold responsible when things are out of order. The woman can walk by sight, but the man cannot. The woman can eat from the fruit, indeed, but the man must remain conscious of the Word of God and the reality of living by that Word.

Accountability

You would think that God would hold the man and woman to the same level of accountability. While as believers we are held to the same standard, in the family the man is held to a higher level of accountability. Let's look at our body. While the feet and arms and other parts of the body are vitally important, they receive tangible direction for operation from the head. It is the same in our families. Headship means being able to be held accountable. As a man, God will measure us by the movement of the family. I will give you an example. One of the scriptures that I used to really have problems with was 1 Peter 3:7. God tells the husband in this verse that based upon how we treat our wives, our prayers can go unanswered. God never tells a woman in the Scriptures that her prayers might not be answered based upon how she treats her husband. Why? Because God holds man accountable in the marriage at a different level. I wonder how many times dreams have gone unachieved and how much potential has been wasted because of how men treated their wives. The next time you hear a man bragging about being called to be the head of the household, remind him about the level of responsibility and accountability required to operate in the office of husband.

Vision

One of the most profound areas of responsibility for a pastor is vision. The Bible declares that "where there is no vision people perish" (Prov. 29:18). *Perish* means "to cast off restraint." Simply stated, we lose when we do not have direction.

When we examine the original marriage, we see God giving Adam the vision and plan for the family. It then becomes Adam's responsibility to communicate and teach the vision to the family. When we discuss submission in the chapters pertaining to the role of the wife, we will develop a greater understanding of the need for vision. Submission does not mean "do everything I say" but really means understanding and yielding to the vision for the family as set forth by the leader. If the husband has not spent time with God to receive a vision for the family, then there is no continuity and concepts to work toward and by which to measure growth. In fact, the husband should be developing a vision for the family in multiple areas. Strategic planning and vision for the family is imperative for the family to remain healthy. The vision should include but not be limited to: finances, health, service, spirituality, and home. Once a vision incorporating these areas is developed, it should be defined by short-range goals, mid-range goals, and long-term goals. Developing a strategic plan and vision for the family allows the growth and progress to be measured and evaluated. This vision should be written and shared with everyone in the family. The vision drives our decisions and provides marching orders for the family. Everyone in the family should understand their role based upon the vision. How do we know where we are going and how we are progressing without a plan and a vision?

Warrior

Several days ago, my son and I were playing a fatherly game of Ping-Pong. It started innocently enough; however, as the game progressed, the spirit of healthy competition began to take control. When the scores finally reached the game-point level, the intensity escalated to a point where we were both lost in the pursuit of victory. Therein lies the spirit of a warrior! Men are wired by God to be warriors and look for a battle. Like a solider trained to fight, a man without a challenge is frustrated.

Men need a fight but unfortunately cannot see the adversary clearly, so they must be directed and focused toward the enemy. Have you ever noticed how men refuse to ask for directions when they are lost? The warrior in them interprets the need for directions as weakness and losing. The role of the wife is to point the enemy out. A good man will fight to overtake him when he is identified.

Every challenge is not a battle to be won.

Perhaps this explains why men are vocal and engaged when their favorite team is playing or their child is on the basketball court or football field playing sports; they are warriors by composition. This concept, which is the crowning reality of a man, can also be a man's most difficult quality to mature through and understand. Because men are warriors, and warriors always look for a fight, many times it becomes hard for a man to handle disagreements without attempting to measure winning and losing. Every encounter for the man can be about winning and losing if he is not trained to understand that every moment should not be measured as combat. This helps us to understand why men can be sore losers. If we measure our value by a won/loss record, we will limit the power of the Holy Spirit to guide and direct us into maturity and greater fellowship with our wives. Every relational encounter is not about destroying our enemy in one-on-one combat. We must remain focused on who the real enemy is. Satan, the great accuser, is our chief enemy and masks himself in multiple disguises and methods.

Spiritual Direction

I am convinced that every man needs a man. Timothy needed a Paul. Elisha had Elijah. Joshua had a Moses. Moses even had Jethro. Every man needs a man to role model manhood for him. From the time little girls are born, they are mentored in the things of family. They play house, change babies, have tea parties, and bake cakes in their play kitchens. Men, on the other hand, are playing games that do not teach them about life—cops and robbers, cowboys and Indians, cars and trucks! By the time a man is ready to get married, he is behind the learning curve in relationship education. Men need men to show them how to walk on the car side of the street with their wife, how to open the car door for their wife, and other qualities that have to be taught and modeled. The world calls this relationship mentoring, but I believe we should call these men "revelation role models." These are the people God can use to be a tangible instrument of the direction and methodology inspired by God for each of us.

Is it not amazing to understand that for almost every other area of our lives we are open to learn and recognize the need for training—except for marriage? We have teachers on our job and in our social activities. And we need teachers for our marriages, also. Young ladies who are moving toward marriage should always ask a few very important questions of their prospective spouse: Who mentored you? Who did you learn how to be a husband from? Who is your life instructor and revelation role model? The basis for these questions is remaining teachable. One of the hardest things for a man, as stated earlier, is yielding and trusting another man to become his teacher and covering. We must rethink and retrain our minds to be open to the principle of covering and instruction.

 If you were to ask women of all age groups, personalities, and economic backgrounds what the greatest need of a woman or wife is, most of them would declare, "Security."

A Wife's Greatest Need

Money, homes, cars, clothes, and other material things are many times thought to be the greatest desires of women when the question is asked of men. While diamonds are a girl's best friend, they are not the greatest need for most women. If you were to ask women of all age groups, personalities, and economic backgrounds what the greatest need of a woman or wife is, most of them would declare, "Security." I have discovered that a woman needs to know that she will have a roof over her and her family's head. Men usually think the woman is more concerned with the size of the house. Women want to have confidence that their husband will do what it takes to keep a roof over them.

The husband is to become the rock that the family can count on. When times are tough, the husband works two jobs. When times are stressful, the husband should broaden his shoulders and seek the wisdom of God. As well, the husband many times has to find other men with whom to share his fears and insecurities. This is no to say that the man should not be free to share with his wife, but at times the leader cannot allow the troops to see his fear.

The husband is the leader. The leader leads the charge, blows the trumpet, and displays confidence in God while wrestling with his personal faith needs and concerns. Please know that the family will sense when the leader's confidence is wavering and weak. The kingdom-minded husband must feed his faith and remain focused in his spirituality, because the adversary is after the family and the first line of family defense is the husband.

Culture has and always will have a great impact on how we think and how we make decisions. In order to have an effective and healthy marital relationship, we must change how we think. The Bible speaks about renewing our minds. When we renew our minds, it will impact other areas of our lives. We must reevaluate our relationships, social environments, and relationship circles. The mind of a husband has to remain focused on the mandate from God on kingdom family leadership. The Bible gives us tremendous insight into how a man must think in relationship to his marriage and his mindset (1 Pet. 3:7). Let's explore how this verse shapes the thinking of a kingdom husband.

A Husband's Presence

In 1 Peter 3, we are reminded that men are to dwell with their wives according to knowledge. The word *dwell* teaches us the value of a man's presence in the home and family. The man is the protector of the household. The faithful and diligent husband protects his family from everything: spiders, frogs, people, the noise outside in the yard, and the loose door on the back porch. Society has forced many men into a keep up with the Joneses mentality, and because they are living beyond their means, many husbands are forced to work many extra hours, which removes them from the home. The presence of a husband in a smaller home has much more impact than the absence of a husband in a larger home.

The word *dwell* has a much more significant meaning when examined closer. When the Bible speaks of a husband dwelling with his wife, it also means "to direct attention." Every wife desires to know that she is a priority in the life of her husband. As a husband, I have found it important to study my wife and understand her need for attention, time, and support. I can always tell when my wife desires time. It shows in her body language and attitude. Time is a commodity that is not redeemable. Time is precious, and we make time for things that are important to us. When I share my time, I make my wife a priority and prove to her that she has value.

A Husband's Preparation

To become a great husband requires becoming a great student. First Peter 3 reminds us to dwell with our wives according to knowledge. The more information I acquire about my wife, the better qualified I am to serve her. I am always amazed at men who do not know their wives' monthly cycles or her shoe size or dress size. I know that my wife likes Nine West shoes. I have educated myself on the style and types of clothing she likes to wear. I can pick up a dress and say, "That looks like Valerie." I attend the University of Valerie and desire to be and remain an honor student.

Knowledge is the missing ingredient for many husbands' ability to be aware and sensitive to the needs of their wives. Is her foot narrow or wide? Does she like long dresses or short ones? For instance, I know that my wife does not like certain style pants. I found this out through studying her. It becomes much easier to satisfy her when I understand her.

When I understand her, it also helps me to handle difficult moments in the relationship. It gives explanation to actions, personality dynamics, and mood swings. I can look at my wife's face and know when she needs a vacation. I can tell when she is angry long before she speaks. I know when she is tired and when she needs her personal space, because I dwell with her according to knowledge. Allow yourself to become such a disciplined student that you have the ability to minister to your wife with greater effect based on your greater understanding of who she is. Ask questions, take notes, watch behavior. Once you begin to study your wife, not only does your relationship grow and develop, but you prevent the adversary from taking a foothold in the relationship and causing division.

A Husband's Practices

When the writer of 1 Peter calls the woman "the weaker vessel," we often misinterpret his point. In 1 Peter 3:7, notice that he really does not say she is weaker; he simply says that the husband is to treat her as though she is weaker. When a man has the flu, he needs to be taken care of as if he were dying. A woman can be sick and still help the kids with homework while cooking dinner—not because of weakness but strength. Women are not weaker but should be *honored* as being weaker. All of this points to the practices of a man. While it might be true that the woman can take out the trash, she should not have to if she is married. Although she can pump gas and change the oil in the car, her husband should treat her as if she cannot. I try not to allow my wife to ever pump gas in her car. This is not pointing to function but rather sensitivity. It does not matter who takes the trash out. It does, however, matter how sensitive I am to my wife not doing certain things. She is strong enough and intelligent enough, but I desire to dwell with her as the weaker vessel and pump the gas myself.

Husbands, please know that when you treat your wife as the weaker vessel, she will not feel inferior or be offended; she will know just how special she is to you. Find ways to illuminate her specialness. Let her know she is precious to you.

A Husband's Promise

Isn't it simply amazing that God places a promise on the husband based upon how he responds to his wife? I really believe that many of the blessings that I have received are because of my wife. In fact, I believe that I am really benefitting from the Lord blessing the faithfulness of my wife. Pharaoh was blessed for Joseph's sake, the Bible declares (Gen. 37:6). Just as that was true for Pharaoh, I believe that men are blessed for their family's sake. A husband has an unusual motivation for serving his wife and family in the order of the Word so that their prayers may not be hindered (1 Pet. 3:7). Notice what the Bible says and does not say. It does not say "so that your prayers will be answered." Instead, it says "not hindered." I learned several years ago that I could release the benefit of my prayer life much sooner by how I treated and responded to my wife. Potentially, my prayer could have already been answered, but the manifestation of the answer might be hindered by my lack of biblical response to my wife.

I cannot help but think about the fact that God must have a sense of humor. Why would He connect my answered prayer with how I serve my wife? This pushes a husband to become more focused and motivated about his relationship with his wife and his role as husband.

Chapter 7

The Model of a Husband

I N THE BOOK OF Deuteronomy, the Bible shares a principle that is important to the life and relationship between a man and a woman as husband and wife. Deuteronomy 24:5 teaches us that a man was not allowed to be sent to the battlefield during his first year of marriage. This is because the kingdom community recognized that building a relational foundation was very important to the continued stability of the marriage. Let's look at four attributes that should be modeled by the kingdom-minded husband.

The Husband Must Be Submissive

A lot is said about the woman being submissive to her husband. Ephesians 5:21, however, teaches that both the husband and the wife are to submit to one another. We can find further examples of the biblical principle of submission in 1 Corinthians 11:3, where it says every man is to be submitted to Christ. A key component in the role and model of a husband is his ability to be submitted to God first. I have discovered that a woman has no problem submitting to a husband who is truly submitted to God. When the husband is submitted to God, he will have no problem submitting to the set leadership of God. As difficult as it is many times for a man to trust a man, we must transform our minds and become committed to the principle of kingdom submission. When we submit to the physical authority of God in the earthly realm, such as our local pastor, we open our lives up to receive the favor of God in the area of our marriage.

 A man in authority is a man under authority.

Being submitted to God means committing to being teachable. God has given us pastors after His heart. God calls the husband to submit himself to the godly direction and correction of the set leadership in the body of Christ. I have witnessed the benefit of godly submission in my personal life. Because of my submission to kingdom authority in the body of Christ, God has released kingdom authority in my personal life and family.

A man in authority is a man under authority. Everyone needs to be submitted to someone. When the husband is under the authority of a local (godly) pastor, it brings the family into the order of God. Just as God is Head of Christ, the pastor becomes the head of the husband. While it can be very difficult for a man to submit to the authority of another man, it is imperative that we understand kingdom order.

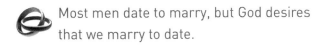 Most men date to marry, but God desires that we marry to date.

The Husband Must Be a Savior

Just as Christ gave Himself for the church, a husband is to give himself for his wife. This is not a physical death but an emotional, spiritual, and social death. Ephesians 5:25 says that Christ gave Himself for the church and that husbands are to love their wives as Christ loved the church. What does it mean to give your life for your wife? The husband should make his wife the priority. She should come first in the order of the home. The husband's priorities should be God, his wife, and then the children. A husband should never be satisfied driving a better car than his wife, wearing nicer clothing, or living at a standard above his wife. The husband should be proud to put himself last in relation to his wife and family. Remember that Christ died a public, painful death for His bride. A kingdom husband should never be ashamed to publicly display making his wife his priority. I love seeing my wife drive the better car and be dressed nicely. Most men date to marry, but God desires that we marry to date.

The kingdom husband has prioritized his life to the point that no one or nothing is more important than his wife. There should be no competition for first place in his life. The greatest gift a man can give his wife is himself. A husband should look beyond her shortcomings and allow her to mature into the woman of destiny she is and become who God has called her to be. Every husband should know and understand that the call to family leadership is a call to sacrifice. I have always liked cars, but understanding the call to marriage has forced me to rethink my need for the newest car on the market. I must be willing to sacrifice my desires for the needs of my family. Educating my children and developing a plan for their future must be my priority. Sacrifice is a cornerstone in the building of marriage and the personal call and responsibility of the husband.

The Husband Must Be a Sanctifier

If Ephesians 5 is a picture of the marital relationship, then another lesson in the model of a husband is the process of sanctifying the wife. When a man gets married, he is called to a life of preparing his wife to please God. The Bible teaches us that Christ sanctified and cleansed the church with the washing of the Word (Eph. 5:26). Therefore, the kingdom husband should be committed to identifying those areas in the life of his wife where spiritual growth is required. The word *sanctify* has ceremonial implications that mean "to make holy or sacred." Find a holy wife, and you should find a husband that has pushed her in understanding her relationship with Christ.

There are mental implications as well. Sanctifying can also mean to respect and charm. When a husband shows behavior that reminds a woman who she is in God, she will bring her life into agreement with that picture. What this means is, treat her like a queen, and she will act like a queen.

We often miss the greatest reward of sanctifying our wives. In Ephesians 5:27 the Bible states that Christ sanctified the church to present her to Himself. Good news, husbands! When I allow God to use me to sanctify my wife, she really becomes a greater gift to me. That's right, just as Eve was a gift to Adam, the wife is a gift from God to the husband. The more diligent I am in serving as a husband, the greater the benefit of a kingdom wife I will receive.

The husband directly receives the benefit of his work as husband and sanctifier. Remember that sanctification is not what is worn, how long the dress is, or how much makeup is or is not worn. Sanctification is growth. It is a process of measured improvement. Each husband must identify areas of concern in behavior and activity in the life of his wife and assist her in changing those areas for the glory of God. A gossiping wife needs to be sanctified in her language. A spending wife needs to be sanctified in her stewardship. While every woman is different, the call remains the same for all husbands. Sanctify her through the Word. Remind her about the Word. Teach her the Word. Model the Word. Sanctification is a continual process in which the Holy Spirit is allowed to change us into the believer who produces much fruit for the kingdom.

The husband is reminded to be a producer of growth in the life of the wife.

The Husband Must Be a Satisfier

One of the hardest areas for a husband can be in the area of satisfaction. I cannot tell you how many times I have heard a man state, "I do not know what she wants." Kingdom husbands are committed to satisfying their wives. I know this can be a difficult pill to swallow for many men, but hear me out, please. Ephesians 5:28 is clear that husbands are to love their wives as their own bodies. Could this be pointing to satisfaction? I believe so. Verse 29 makes it clearer. It shares that no man hates his own flesh; but, "nourisheth and cherisheth it." The word *nourisheth* means "to suckle, flow, or promote growth." Once again, the husband is reminded to be a producer of growth in the life of the wife. However, the word *suckle* gives some clarity on how the feeding and growth are to take place. *Suckle* implies that the feeding is produced through a close relationship with her husband. Let me try to give you an example. My wife has never gone to seminary, but because of her close relationship with me, she is able to grasp and use seminary terms and has developed a keen eye for scriptural revelation and teaching. It can be said that I have nurtured her growth in understanding theological concepts and perspectives. The wife should be able to feed off the personal spiritual growth of the husband. That is why the husband must maintain spiritual healthiness.

When we think about cherishing something, several thoughts come to mind. *Cherish* means "to harbor in the mind deeply or to feel with affection." This really points to the emotional and mental component of the husband's responsibility to his wife.

She must be on his mind and in his thoughts. Time must be given to reflection and meditation in order to become more effective in the role of husband. Many times it is only God who can reveal the needs of a wife to her husband. Cherishing can also remind us to handle our wives with care. They are precious. They are gifts from God, valuable and breakable. When we place high value on our wives, we will think twice before engaging in behavior that can cause harm to our relationship. You can tell the value of something by how it is treated and cared for. I submit that many husbands have failed to place proper value on their wives.

In my home, I do not pay any bills and have very little day-to-day involvement in the financial business of our home. That has caused me to place unusually high value on my wife. She is my lover, partner, accountant, and so many other things. I cannot afford for her to be sick. I need her healthy. I work hard to provide a life for her that ensures her longevity. I must take her on vacations. I need her to get her rest because she is valuable to me. I help with the assignments of the home because I want her around. We have a housekeeper because I want her around. I need her. I recognized early in our marriage that life without her would be a struggle. The old saying is true: when my wife is happy, the whole house is happy.

Husbands must commit themselves to becoming a satisfier. It does not mean that everything a wife desires is provided, but it does mean that sensitivity to the value of the wife is clear. I want my wife to know that she is important.

Chapter 8

How Women Are Wired

WOMEN AND MEN ARE wired so differently that it becomes difficult for them to understand each another without developing a tremendous sensitivity to the very differences that attract men and women. God created men and women and placed in each of them those components necessary for the completion of their assignments. Because the callings are different, the wiring is different. If we can learn to understand and appreciate our differences, then we can benefit from those differences in marriage. As hard as it is to understand the opposite sex, it would be much more difficult to live with them if they were wired in the same way that we are.

Women Are Circular

How many times have you observed a disagreement between a husband and wife, and the wife was reminding the man about a previous situation? Their accounts are often totally different, and the details are not even closely related. Women, by nature, are capable of recalling details with greater accuracy because they process in a circle. That is why when most men have forgotten the details from previous situations, a woman can not only remember the details, but accurately shares details about time, place, and people. Men are not forgetful; they just recall information differently. A woman can remember the color and dress style she had on several Sundays ago. Men cannot remember the suit that they wore to church last Sunday.

Because women operate with a circular personality, it many times becomes harder for them to move on after situations. While many men can let go and begin to move forward without looking back, women have to move beyond triggers that can push them into a state of reflection and remorse. Please do not misunderstand, I am not suggesting that women should learn how to change this behavior, I am simply giving clarity about why the behavior exists. Men must be aware that breaking a woman's trust will be harder to recover from because they reflect and remember at a different level than men. Women can remember what they were given for an anniversary present for the last several years. Men normally cannot remember what they received for their anniversary last year. It is the reflection and remembrance abilities that can cause great difficulty in understanding each other in marriage.

Women Are Disciplined

I must remind you that there are always exceptions to every rule, but usually women are more disciplined than men. The proof can be seen when walking around the average home. How many projects have been started by men and have yet to be finished, like the half-painted privacy fence, the unfinished storage shed? Because women tend to be more disciplined, they usually are task oriented. My wife plans the day for grocery shopping and other family responsibilities based upon prices and crowds. She has predetermined the best time of day to do the shopping and very rarely needs to stop during the week for spontaneous grocery shopping.

Men must recognize this when planning for family events

and other relational situations. When a woman plans a night out, she takes care of all issues, from the location of the movie to the babysitter. Women get frustrated when the same level of detail is not provided for them. Men will plan the date but not secure a babysitter or look in the paper for movie times. In order to understand women, men must learn to be more sensitive to details. Notice the new dress, write down notes about past experiences and celebrations, and make mental notes about the details of the planned date, For men, developing an appreciation for details can assist in the growth of our marital relationships. Paying attention to details can pay dividends that will be appreciated by both husband and wife.

Women Are Multitaskers

Men typically are one-thing-at-a-time people. Women, on the other hand, can handle multiple tasks at the same time. Perhaps the greatest reason women need to be detailed driven is because of their ability to multitask. God has placed within most women the ability to focus on several things at the same time. This can, many times, be the single most evident source of frustration for a woman. Because she has the ability to accomplish multiple tasks, she can see progress in completing family assignments and responsibilities. While this particular attribute is tremendous, it can also lead to stress and burnout. The challenge for many women is finding a healthy balance.

My wife often shares with the women in our church to resist the pressure to be a "superwife." The dishes, the cooking, the homework, and many other responsibilities can all come tumbling down like a brick wall. Unless your husband is different, he really does not care about many of the details that are stressing you. For the overall health of the relationship, the multitasking wife must learn how to prioritize. While all men are not the same, most men would rather their wife make intimacy a priority over the dinner dishes. Putting household responsibilities into a manageable process of prioritizing will provide a much healthier attitude and atmosphere for the family. Just because women can multi-task does not mean it is always healthy to do so.

Women Are Warring

When we examine Genesis and look at the portrait of Eve, we understand that God placed within the woman an unusual spirit of warring. While men are warriors, women are warring. As stated earlier, men cannot usually see the enemy, but women can. Not only are women equipped to see the enemy, but they have been wired with little tolerance for the enemy. Women do not handle foolishness well. Women can come out to the church for a prayer breakfast and leave not speaking because of this fact. The eggs could have been prepared perfectly, but the lady who prepared the eggs might have a contrary spirit. Women pick up on those types of things and call them out. Perhaps this is because, according to the Bible, God put enmity between the woman's seed and the seed of the adversary. The word *enmity* really means "hatred." Women hate the adversary. Women, therefore, are sensitive to the plans and plots of the enemy in ways a man cannot be.

When I hire staff, I like to introduce them to my wife early on in the process because she can see what is not visible. Women have a spiritual eye that is keen and sharp. They can look into the eyes of an individual and see into their soul. How many times have you observed a woman having a "feeling" about something before it is revealed? This warring spirit can pose great problems, however, if left unchecked and not properly stewarded. Women must govern this ability and allow the Holy Spirit to teach them how to be sensitive to handling situations and people. A quick tongue can bring disaster to relationships and take years to repair. Just because you have the ability to see the adversary's plan does not always mean you are called or equipped to respond. The disciplined woman understands how to seek the direction of God and move under the control of the Spirit. Every enemy is not to be conquered. The undisciplined woman can leave a trail of broken people behind, all in the name of kingdom work and ministry.

Once again we see the value of marriage and the great plan of God. The warring woman should make clear the plan of the adversary so that her warrior husband can go fight the battle. To allow the relationship of the husband and wife to work in concert this way will manifest a great witness for the kingdom while destroying the reign of the adversary in the lives of our families.

Women Process on the Spot

Here is an example of a decision-making scenario. A decision must be made about daycare for the baby. A woman gathers information about daycare centers, shares the information with her husband, and desires a selection. Here is the problem! She wants the decision now. Women do not usually take a long time to make decisions, while men do. Women can usually process the information, make a decision, and move on. As well, women usually misinterpret the man's response as being insensitive and uncaring if he does not make a decision on the spot. Men are not insensitive, just different.

It goes without saying that there is a great difference between the sexes. Neither is better than the other, but it is of great benefit for each to be understood in light of their differences. It does not usually take a woman as long to make a decision because that is how God has wired them. Why do you think God wired them that way? Perhaps if a woman processed the way a man does, nothing would ever get done or the family vision would never take place. When a husband shares the vision for the family, the woman usually has a lot of questions because she is moving very quickly to a point of decision. Give her the information, communicate it clearly, and she will decide. I believe that God wires men and women differently in this area for the production of family vision. Men take it personally when the woman appears to question his plan. We are called to understand and appreciate our differences. These differences make our lives beneficial and our goals achievable.

 A husband sees only a cookout. A wife sees table locations, types of cups, and numbers of hot dogs.

Women See the Big Picture

Thank God that women can see the larger picture when making decisions, while men tend to see only today. Women see the future and the implications of the decisions of today and their impact on tomorrow. When a man has a vision, it is black and white. A great wife carries with her colored pencils to make the vision of her man more than just a sketch. Because women are able to see a larger picture, they can add color to the dreams of men that men would never be able to see and develop. A husband sees only a cookout. A wife sees table locations, types of cups, and numbers of hot dogs.

While men might have a great idea, it is the big-picture, vision thinking of a woman that sometimes causes stress in the marriage. Whenever a husband shares a vision with his wife, he must be prepared to answer many questions. Because she has the ability to see beyond the decisions of the day, questions must be raised and answered, and that can many times cause the man to feel unsupported in pursuing the vision. I would dare suggest that striking a balance in how we develop vision can make the roles of husband and wife vitally important. When husbands and wives partner their abilities, the end result can be a very productive process of making decisions. Someone must see the big picture in order to answer valuable questions and prevent unforeseen problems and difficulties.

Close examination of the differences between how men and women think continually points to the divine planning of our Creator and His desire that marriage be a corporation of abilities that has great impact on our society. The visionary needs a big-picture person to process, plan, and develop the required steps to manifesting vision and insuring critical success.

Women must remain sensitive to the way in which they respond to the ideas and vision of their husband. It is true—the male ego is extremely fragile. A soft word joined with a sensitive tone can prove to be an invaluable combination in creating an atmosphere of teamwork and productivity. Husbands must come to understand that because of our differences, women will have questions. Questions should not be interpreted as a lack of support but as an opportunity to be successful. Questions produce thinking, and thinking produces success.

Women Are Idealistic

One of the greatest differences between men and women is how they process the concept of life in general. It was stated earlier than men are visual and are compelled by what they see. Women are idealists and are driven by concepts and dreams.

Women have concepts of success that are very different from those of men. Many times I have had men tell me that they did not even know that their marriage was in trouble because they were measuring the marriage by what they drove and where they lived. Women measure the marriage by the atmosphere in the home and other conceptual, nonverbal components.

Women are impressed with the man who works, not necessarily with the job he works. Women are impressed with the thought of flowers more than the type of flowers. One flower purchased at the cash register carries as much clout as a dozen roses when presented with the understanding of the conceptual implications of the thought behind the flowers. Too many times, men do not place enough value on attempting to understand the mental picture and not just the physical picture.

A man walking in the door from work covered in dirt can have a greater impact on a woman than a man entering the house in shorts with an athletic build. The concept of the working man is provision. A letter written on a napkin placed under her pillow carries more weight than roses purchased from a florist many times. The influence of media has had a great impact on these concepts and ideas. Because men are visual, they tend to get lost in the tangible and pay little attention to the intangible. I can bring home a favorite candy bar and impact the life of my wife to a much greater extent than with a very expensive dress or a box of candy. Concepts speak loudly. A daily cell phone call, an impromptu lunch date, a note detailing the filling up of the gas tank in the car are all conceptual ways in which a man can impact his marriage and develop a greater relationship with his wife. Turning on the coffee maker without being asked presents a mental picture to the wife about her value in the eyes of her husband. Remember that many times what she says nonverbally is louder than what she might say verbally.

Details, Details, Details

My imagination is filled with examples that explain how women communicate details. Let's try this one. When a woman has a flat tire on the side of the road, she calls her husband. She usually will begin by telling him too many details. For instance, she will tell him who is riding with her, where they were going, the sound the tire made when it went flat, how long they have been on the side of the road, how many cars have passed without helping, and which tire is flat. The husband really only wants to know two things: is she OK, and where is she? The husband becomes frustrated because he has to process through all the details before he can make decisions related to fixing the tire. During the process of communication, it helps if we can remember how men and women process information and train our behavior to become more sensitive to our differences. Women must learn how to reduce the amount of details and give only those pieces of information that are pertinent and required to address the situation. Men lose their focus in too many details. They have short fuses and can become frustrated. Since a man usually has a short listening capacity, women should steward the time of communication with a keen awareness that limited details are required.

Chapter 9

The Role of the Wife

J̲UST AS G̲OD GAVE the man a title in marriage called *husband*, He gave the woman a title called *wife*. But it is interesting to realize that God added another description to the woman's title—*helpmeet*. Growing up in church, I always heard this term referred to as "help mate." Only upon close examination of Scripture during my adult life did I realize the term was being misused. The wife is called to be a helpmeet. Simply stated, she has a dual call from God to help and to meet. Have you ever noticed that most churches have more women engaged in ministry than men? I suggest to you that it is because women have a God-given component that compels them to want to help make something happen.

 Men are called to dream. Women are called to help make dreams happen.

HelpMeet

Women must always have a vision, project, goal, or objective to pursue. When a woman is married to a man who has no dreams and ambitions, she can become very frustrated. Men are called to dream. Women are called to help make dreams happen. Many times in our marriages a great source of stress is found in the fact that a husband shares his vision with everyone except his wife. God has created the marriage union to provide a corporate vehicle for teamwork and completion of assignments that are vital to the destiny of a man and his wife. Once we are married, we no longer have dual destinies but one corporate destiny. The success that I have attained in ministry is a direct result of the order of my marriage. Before I share a ministry vision with anyone, I share it with my wife. She is equipped by the Spirit to bring a voice of revelation to my dreams and visions like no one else. Society has trained and equipped men to think that they need no help from anyone; however, God has given us a great asset in our wives.

When a wife understands that being a helpmeet is part of her call and destiny, she can understand the dreams of her husband with new excitement. She must be committed to finding her place and role in relation to the dreams and visions of the family, while the husband must understand her value and call in relation to assisting or helping with the manifestation of the dreams. Being a helper means participation. While it can be frustrating for a woman to see her husband with a dream in which she is not invited to participate, it can be equally frustrating to see him going after dreams that are not God's will for the family. When a husband has a vision from God, the abilities of the wife should produce confirmation about the dream. In short, if the gifts and abilities of the wife do not line up with the needs of the vision, then there is the need to resurvey the vision. My wife, Valerie, has tremendous gifts in accounting and management. She has become an unbelievable help in manifesting the vision that God has given me for the church and ministry that I lead. Without her, the dreams would not be a reality.

Not only is the wife a helper, but her God-given title speaks of the fact that she is called to meet. What then is the wife called to meet? With any vision there is the gap between revelation and manifestation. This gap can become overwhelming to a man with little patience and stamina. As stated earlier, women are usually stronger and able to endure stress much better than men. God has wired them that way. Women are equipped to assist their husbands in closing the gap and remaining committed and faithful to the vision. Much of the ministry stress that could become a distraction for me is handled by my wife. She handles it with less stress and greater focus. Focus, faithfulness, and stamina are requirements of seeing any vision reach manifestation. Therefore, the role of a wife in this process is vital. When a woman understands the role of meeting, she looks for those times and situations that discourage a man. She will then use one of her greatest gifts, discernment, to encourage her husband at critical moments in the process of pursuing a dream.

The wife also must understand how to meet the husband in the process itself. By this, I mean learning how to share your perspectives, concerns, and ideas without overshadowing him. A wife who has learned this lesson understands how to share the idea but not claim the glory for the idea. She can allow her husband to receive the glory for those things that were originally her idea and concept. A godly wife is not concerned with headlines but accomplishment. The Bible teaches us that a godly woman becomes excited about her husband becoming well known in the gates of the city (Prov. 31:23). Her joy is in the success of the family and its God-given destiny. Even when the husband and wife cannot agree, the wife after God's heart has learned how to "meet" her husband. She understands the need for compromise and remembers that God will ultimately hold the man accountable for the vision. Knowing that he is accountable to God should be enough to keep the husband focused, but overcoming the frustration of pushing toward a kingdom vision can become easier with a wife who can help him meet the qualifications and responsibilities required to achieve vision success.

 When men allow their wives to help and when women allow their husbands to lead, they become a powerful instrument for kingdom building.

Wives must remain open to helping and meeting throughout the process of going after the things of God with her husband. The combination of leadership from the husband and helping from the wife is very powerful. They become a team that is hard to stand against. When men allow their wives to help, and when women allow their husbands to lead, they become a powerful instrument for kingdom building. This is not to say that women do not have the ability to manifest vision, but their vision should line up with and support the vision of the husband. Visions have many components, but there can only be one overall vision, while it might include multiple subset visions. We often hear the church talk about submission, but there must also be *sub-vision*.

Identifying and Defining the Enemy

As we shared earlier, the difference between men and women is that women are warring while men are warriors. For a moment, let's focus on Adam and Eve and their fall from the garden. When we study this story, we can clearly define the roles and where the breach allowing the entry of Satan took place. Adam was not the original inhabitant of the garden, but Satan was. Satan fell from heaven, according to the Bible. The serpent in the garden was the original inhabitant, and Adam was placed in the garden and given dominion over everything, including the serpent. Adam is called to have authority over the Earth and everything that is in and on the Earth. The Bible gives us a vital component of anthropological revelation when it says, "It is not good for man to be alone" (Gen. 2:18, author's paraphrase). Man has a need that cannot be fulfilled without the presence of a woman. I cannot tell you how many times my wife has been able to identify Satan long before I could.

Women have a call of identification. Husbands need wives to identify Satan. Adam had been living in the garden unaware of the presence of Satan. There is no recorded conversation between Adam and the serpent. This does not point to the fact that Adam was not capable of talking to the serpent, but rather that maybe Adam did not know the serpent existed. The creation and presence of Eve changes all this. Eve is capable of seeing the adversary. This gift, however, goes unrecognized and not properly used by Adam and Eve. Once Eve was aware of the adversary, rather than communicating with him she should have communicated with Adam. Perhaps we have stumbled on to a biblical principle of communication. When the process of communication between the husband and wife is closed, the adversary will take advantage and open lines of communication himself. Women need to talk, and they will find someone to talk to. Communication between Adam and Eve would have precluded her desire to talk with the serpent. The adversary takes advantage of the fact that the wife desires communication. I am not suggesting that a wife without communication will seek communication with the adversary. But we can be clear that a wife needs communication vitally and will become vulnerable during a time when communication is not open and available.

Eve did not seek the adversary. The adversary sought Eve based upon his knowledge of how she was wired. Satan understands us better than we understand ourselves. When the husband is not aware of the importance of communication, he makes her spiritually vulnerable. The adversary simply takes advantage of the opportunity to produce division. If Adam and Eve had been communicating properly, Eve would not have entertained conversation with the serpent. Instead, when she recognized the serpent, she would have communicated his presence with Adam. Although much has been said about Adam and Eve and the serpent, I have never really held to the concept that Eve made a critical error in judgment. I believe they did not understand their roles and the importance of communication. Much will be said about this in the chapter on communication.

Eve, the warring wife, was equipped with identification skills that Adam did not have. Eve should have returned to Adam and introduced him to the reality of the presence of the serpent. This is true because when God asked Adam what has happened, he only identified the presence of the woman. He was unaware that the serpent existed. One of the greatest roles of a wife is the identification of the enemy. Whether it is a woman on the job, a child with bad influence over the children of the family, or a friend that has the ability to sow negative influence in the life of her husband, a woman has the ability to see and point to the serpent. The husband needs to know where and how the enemy moves and fights. Once again we see a picture of the teamwork that God desires between the husband and the wife. When the kingdom husband understands this concept he becomes capable of pursuing the enemy with new passion and success.

Another part of identifying the adversary is not simply location, but operation. Women have the ability to observe and discern the operations, methods, and processes of the adversary. Ultimately Satan is a liar, but he employs many strategies in his process of attacking the family. Just as the presence of the adversary is usually invisible to the man, the operations of the adversary are equally invisible. The godly wife must learn to employ her gifts and abilities to properly channel her anointing during these times. Because of the enmity God has placed between the adversary and the woman, wives many times want to destroy the enemy themselves. We must be committed to remembering our roles in marriage. The husband is the warrior and is equipped to actually fight. The role of the warring wife is to encourage her husband during the battle, motivate him during tough battles, and celebrate him when the victory has been accomplished. Women who attempt to identify and fight the battle run the risk of overstepping their bounds of gifting, as well as impacting the ego of their warrior husband. Remember that every man needs an enemy to fight. The role of the wife is to give him a foe. When the wife fails to produce a foe, the man many times seeks out or manufactures an enemy. When the enemy is correctly identified and the husband is released to do battle, the family will survive and become the vehicle for extensive kingdom building in our society.

A Husband's Greatest Need

One of the most broken theories about marriage is based upon the needs of men. Most people share that a man's greatest need is sexual satisfaction. That is a theory promoted and manipulated by the media and our culture. In actuality, perhaps the greatest need of a man is to be needed. My wife often shares with other women that they need to learn how to become more vulnerable. The kingdom-minded wife understands that men have a rescue mentality. They need to know that their presence is valuable and needed. They need to be a savior. Many times, when a husband is involved in an extramarital affair, it had nothing originally to do with intimacy and sex. It usually begins with the other woman making him feel valuable.

The strong, independent woman who can fix everything can also have the most difficulty understanding how to allow her husband to fix the broken door or to hang the picture on the wall. This becomes even more difficult to handle when married to a man who procrastinates. But remember that many times fixing the broken pipe can be more of a blow to family peace than leaving it broken. As well, hiring someone else to fix it can also be intimidating to the man with weak and low masculine self-esteem.

Men love being the hero. Sisters, tell them how grateful you are when they fix something. Stroke that male ego. Encourage that great male pride. Even those husbands who are not handy around the house should be given opportunity to lead the initiative to have the home repairs completed. I hear women all over asking at this moment, What happens when the husband moves too slowly to accomplish the needed tasks? Can I suggest that those women allow the husband to give them direction about choosing the professionals required to accomplish the tasks? Regardless of how the circumstances present themselves, men need to feel valued. A man who feels needed will eventually rise to new levels and become the family leader required by God to bring the family into new levels of strength and success.

Chapter 10

The Wife's Job Description

W E HAVE ALREADY DETERMINED that the woman is by nature an equipping helper to the husband. This means that she makes life easier and has something necessary for the success of the vision that God places in the heart of the man. In Genesis 2:18 the Bible declares that God created the woman as a helper. This means that she has been wired with the needs of a specific man in mind and not every man. A man is called to a destiny search, seeking the woman that God has ordained to be his helper. She has specific attributes that are required for his assignment. Perhaps the first step to finding a wife is acknowledging our weaknesses. This will point us to the attitudes and strengths required in a wife. She is a helper and therefore should not necessarily have the same strengths and attributes of her husband. She is a plus where he is a minus and a minus where he is a plus.

The Helper's Confidence

The word *help* has a primitive root that means "surround." In fact, the job description of a wife is to identify those areas in her husband's persona that are weak and vulnerable and cover those areas. Covering him in these areas does not imply ignoring weaknesses or covering them up but bringing to the relationship tools that enable him to still be productive and successful in spite of these areas. She helps him to address his areas of weakness in order to overcome them.

The kingdom wife must remain very confident in the fact that she is a very important part of the healthy movement and development of the family. She is more than just a child bearer; she is equipped to fill in the blanks and make everyone around her better. In short, she is an improver. Another way of identifying the importance of a wife is for her to see herself as a counterpart. When God created the woman, He took a rib from the chest and side of Adam (Gen. 2:21). Theologically this points to the idea that a part of man is missing until he finds his wife. When a man finds his wife, a missing part is returned and placed back in position and an unusual completeness is found. Therefore, the woman must maintain confidence in her role based upon the fact that God equipped her perfectly. She must remind herself that everything God needed her to posses was placed within her before the foundation of world. In fact, marriage is more than the coming together of two people; it is really the coming together of two destinies to complete kingdom assignments on the Earth.

The Helper's Spirituality

Although everything a husband needs from his wife is already placed in her, it does not automatically manifest and create an environment for success. The kingdom wife needs spiritual insight on how to release her gifts and how to mange them. This requires investment in her relationship with God. While both husbands and wives need to spend individual time with God, they really have different objectives. Of course, personal spiritual growth and relationship development should always be the primary reason for spending time working on our spirituality; however, there are other reasons as well. For the husband, he must spend time with God to receive vision for the family. The wife must spend time with God to receive direction about the releasing of her gifts and abilities.

Have you ever noticed that the woman is created just after man is given a command from God? In Genesis 2:16, Adam is commanded not to eat from the tree of life, and in verse 18 God says it is not good for man to be alone. Could it be that God understood that man would not be disciplined enough to make spirituality a priority?

A wife who understands her role can assist God in keeping her husband spiritually grounded. This is done not by nagging and pushing but by modeling. One of the greatest instruments a woman possesses is the gift of influence. It is the influence of Eve that leads Adam to eat the fruit. Women have been magnificently wired with influence. This gift is dangerous when not properly yielded to the Holy Spirit. It can be very easily transitioned into manipulation. How many times have you seen a woman wrap a man around her finger because of this? Even my daughters recognize that they can have great influence over me as their father. Wives must yield to spiritual growth in order to ensure the correct release of influence in the life of their husbands. While it is not good for a man to be alone, a man married to a woman who does not manage her influence in line with the will of God can become desperately broken. The old saying is correct: "A woman can make or break a man, because she has a God-given ability to influence him to action." I pray that all women will use this gift to the glory of God and remain sensitive to the ability to influence the kings and priests in their lives.

The Helper's Personality

A man must be able to trust his wife with his secrets. This is, indeed, an earned privilege because men do not share their hearts with just anyone. When a man has trust in his wife, he will have no problem sharing his deepest and most profound thoughts with her. Proverbs 31:10 teaches us how important it is for a man to have trust in his wife's ability to be a confidant. In fact, that scripture shares that the husband will have no lack. The implication is that a man's success is connected to his ability to share his heart with his wife. Let me ask you a question. Where did the bone that created Eve come from? Not his head, not his feet, but his side. Eve was created from a rib. What do ribs do? They protect the heart and other vital organs. Women are ribs. The kingdom wife should have a personality that allows her to receive her husband's thoughts and passion and protect them.

A woman who cannot be trusted will find her husband seeking others to share his dreams with. It is vitally important for every wife to know that just as it is hard for a husband to re-earn trust, it becomes very difficult for a man to trust a wife who has communicated his deepest secrets to others. Men usually breach trust with affairs because someone lends an ear, while women breach trust with talking. Girl talk is dangerous. While the wife might think she is having casual conversation, the releasing of her husband's dreams can prove detrimental to the continued ability for him to have uncompromising trust in her.

Once a woman is married, she must be aware that she cannot talk to everyone and listen to everyone. In fact, she must become sensitive even to whom she listens. Is that not the very thing that unravels Adam and Eve's destiny? She listened to the wrong source. Kingdom wives should operate with a personality that enables them to release their husbands to operate with a liberty that allows him to share whatever he needs to with her. Although I run the risk of turning women off everywhere with my next statement, I will take that risk. Sometimes the greatest hindrance to women being trusted by their husbands is found in the communicative relationships of those women who are close to them. Sisters, mothers-in-law, and mothers can prove to be the very women who become instruments of breaching trust. If a husband wanted those women to know his deepest thoughts and fears, he would have shared them himself. He wants to share them with his wife, his helper, his partner, and her only.

The Helper's Priority

Because women are creative at multi-tasking, it is important for them to remain focused and set proper priorities in their roles as helpmeets to their husbands. Genesis 2:20 helps to bring clarity to the priority of a wife. When Adam named all the animals, the Bible declares that there was not found a companion suitable for him. Every other creature had a companion except Adam. God therefore saw a need in the life of Adam and created woman to meet that need. When I perform marriage ceremonies, I remind the congregation that God put Adam asleep and created and fashioned Eve while he was asleep. While most people would think Adam was put asleep because of the taking of the rib from his side, please allow me to suggest another concept. I believe that God knew exactly what Adam needed in a wife and did not desire input from Adam about Eve. God knew her size, shape, intellect, and all other characteristics that were required to fulfill the needs of Adam and his destiny. God gave Adam the privilege of naming Eve but did not allow him to have input into her creation. She was a gift from God to Adam to assist in his destiny and kingdom assignment. She was suited for him.

I love buying suits, but interestingly enough, suits are not "one size fits all." They are personally fitted. I wear a forty long. While I can wear other sizes, they will not be likely to fit properly. Women are only equipped to be suited to their husband, and that must become one of their priorities in life. That is why it can be dangerous to seek advice from all women; they are not suited to your situation and your husband.

Remember that Eve did not exist until Adam needed a companion. The word *companion* comes from two words, *with* and *bread*. Therefore, a priority for the woman is to be with her husband. In short, this means that there must be a time investment from the wife. She must spend time learning to understand how he thinks and to recognize the red flags in his life. What are those things that push him away and those things that draw him closer? By understanding her priority to be the bread in his life, she will learn how to feed him. Bread is a staple in the food system. The kingdom wife must make consistency a priority. When she has proven that she can be trusted through all types of circumstances, she will be blessed to truly become a partner in the life of her husband. When she proves to be a secret keeper, trusted listener, and quiet advisor, she will be released into new levels of relational satisfaction and feel tremendous personal fulfillment as a wife called of God.

Chapter 11

The Submissive Wife

T HIS CHAPTER INVOLVES DIALOGUE about what has become a filthy word in modern society, *submission*. For whatever reason, God, our Creator, decided before the foundation of the world that man should be the head of the household. In an earlier chapter on the role of the husband, we made it clear that it does not necessarily mean that man was the most qualified. God simply needed to establish order, authority, responsibility, and accountability. Therefore, Ephesians 5:22 was established as the *Magna Carta* of marriage, the rule of operation and standard operating procedure for couples to govern themselves by. Ephesians 5:22 reminds us that wives are to submit themselves to their husbands. While submission has been misunderstood and manipulated, clear understanding of the concept can inspire believers to become better stewards of one of the most precious gifts given to man and woman—a kingdom marriage.

 First, a woman is to submit unto her *own* husband. And secondly, *they* are to submit as unto Christ.

The Mind of Submission

When one thinks of the mindset that must be developed in order to fully establish a perspective of submission, two things are related in Scripture. First, a woman is to submit unto her *own* husband. And secondly, *they* are to submit as unto Christ. What could God have meant when He said, "Submit…as unto the Lord" (Eph. 5:22)? Could it be that submission should be the result of a husband who has first yielded himself to the order of the kingdom? Remember that our Lord Jesus was fully submitted unto the Godhead, His Father. In fact, Christ often shared that He could only do what His Father sent Him to do. When a husband is committed to operating in the order of the Word and displays a lifestyle that examplifies his submission to God, the wife is called to respond with submission to her husband. "As unto Christ," really means that the husband should respond to God as Christ did, inspiring the wife to submit to him. I have observed, however, that many times women who have been believers longer than their husbands have difficulty submitting to them fully upon their desire to receive Christ. The key to submission is recognizing that you do not always have to agree or understand all decisions in order to submit. The mind of submission is based upon the confidence of a wife in the fact that her husband is being led by God. I often remind men that this level of trust is earned through consistent evidence of spiritual growth. A husband who has proven his relationship with Christ will not have to worry about his wife not submitting unto him.

 It is never acceptable to follow anyone when a call to compromise the Word is required.

The Model of Submission

The word *submission* itself can give us deep insight into what God intended when He said wives were to submit themselves unto their husbands. The prefix *sub-* means "under." So the model of submission is not the loss of identity but actually the finding of purpose and destiny. When a man finds a wife, and she submits unto him, she does not lose herself but actually finds herself. Her mission really becomes a mission under his mission. It is not a separate mission but a stabilizing mission.

I am often asked if it is required of a woman to submit to a husband that is not saved. The answer is yes, but some clarification is required. First Peter 3:3–6 teaches us that wives are to be in subjection to their husbands even if they do not obey the Word. In that case, it can be the very submission of the wife that wins the husband to the kingdom. We must make it clear that submission does not mean following her husband or anyone else contrary to the Word. It is never acceptable to follow anyone when a call to compromise the Word is required. Every believer is called to have solitary commitment to Christ as their Lord and Savior. However, the fact that a husband is not saved does not release the wife from the principle of submission in the sense of the establishment of the home. Much can be said about not marrying the unsaved person from the beginning, which is clearly shared in the Word. But many times, what has taken place is that one person has accepted Christ after being married, placing the marriage in an unequally yoked context. When this is the case, the saved woman is still called to submission. In this case, it will be the principles, actions, and behaviors of the saved spouse that will be used for the Lord through the Holy Spirit to lead the unsaved spouse into relationship with Christ.

Perhaps the greatest two ways that a woman can inspire her husband to change are through words and witness. Too many times the husband does not see the evidence of change and sanctification in his wife, and therefore he does not come under the authority of conviction to change. When the kingdom wife governs her actions and words while modeling the behavior of a believer, she will find God moving upon the heart of her husband, and he will soon be following her to worship.

The Method of Submission

Now that we have established what submission is and how the wife should think and act, let's consider the process that she can use in manifesting a spirit of submission in her marriage. The first six verses of 1 Peter 3 help us to understand the very methods that God desires a wife use to become sensitive, too. Phrases like "chaste conversation coupled with fear" and "the hidden man of the heart" suggest that this methodology really begins with the internal composition of a woman and not the external existence. In short, the method is to work on the spirit woman more than the carnal woman. The inside is more valuable than the outside. A woman should watch what she says and how she says it. While hair, makeup, lipstick, and clothing are important to the visual stimuli for a man, women must not forget they can be beautiful outside and ugly on the inside.

 When a woman can control her words and pick them with sensitivity, she embraces the methods of submission that God anoints.

The methods of submission are engulfed in learning how to govern your mouth. When a woman can control her words and pick them with sensitivity, she embraces the methods of submission that God anoints. The tongue of a woman can be deadly when not governed properly. That same passage found in 1 Peter 3 actually goes on to say that women are to follow the example of Sarah, who called Abraham her lord. This means the method of submission is to be founded in attempting to please her husband. A wife should dress for her husband, not the other women on the job or at the church. When she makes her husband lord, it does not imply heresy but perspective. After pleasing God, pleasing her husband should become her priority. Wearing his favorite clothing of hers, cooking his favorite meal, and watching the game with him are all ways in which a wife can call her husband lord. Speaking positively to him and about him also call him lord. Women must watch how and with whom they share the imperfections of their husband.

Comparing him to the pastor or reminding him repeatedly about his shortcomings are surefire ways to short circuit marital relationships. In fact, many men simply want to know that when they get it wrong, they will not have to live with the reminder cloud over their heads forever. While we all must be accountable for our mistakes, our mistakes must be weighed properly. There is, in fact, a great difference between moral mistakes and ideological mistakes. Most men know deep down that they do not "run" the house, but the anointed wives know how to let the man think that he does.

The Miracle of Submission

I believe that miracles still exist today. In fact, many times, miracles are right in front of us and we miss them by looking for something larger in the sky. One of the greatest miracles I have witnessed since being in ministry is what can happen in a marriage when the wife commits to living and refining her ability to submit to the kingdom authority of her husband. First Peter 3:2 reminds the wife that her behavior can win her husband. I believe that submission is one of the vital tools God has given women to use, along with their gifts of influence. Remember that husbands watch and notice their wives even when it is not evident. In fact, the word *behavior* can mean "to make stare or take a close look at." Therefore, when a wife learns how to submit to her husband, she forces him to notice her. She commands his attention. When she can respond to him in the order of the kingdom, even when he might not deserve it, she releases the power of the Holy Spirit to move.

When my wife wakes up and does her devotional, she pushes and convicts me to examine my relationship with God without ever speaking words to me. Her actions compel me to aspire to reach new levels in my personal spiritual growth. She becomes a tangible, touchable example that will not allow me to remain or become stagnant. Wives, submit yourselves unto your own husbands, and observe the miracle-working power of God to use you as an agent of the kingdom. Women are powerful. Their influence is great. While waiting on miracles, we perhaps could have the greatest opportunity to witness one in our marriage through the ability of a wife to submit. After all, miracles are what we can expect to happen when we are open and yielded to the possibilities of God.

Chapter 12

Communication

A S I WRITE, OUR nation is preparing for a transfer from analog to digital broadcasting. We have come a long way from the days of rabbit ears on the top of our televisions. Today, we have flat screen and plasma televisions. When I was a child, we had only three television channels, but with the development of cable television, we now have access to hundreds of channels at our fingertips. The key to receiving all of these channels is the ability to receive the signal. The signal is readily available, but only to those who have a digital receiver are capable of accepting and receiving the signal. All forms of communication operate on the principle of transmission and reception. If you have two transmitters, you cannot move the communication between them—one must be a transmitter, while the other must receive.

Walkie-Talkie

When I was a child one of the most popular gifts you could receive at Christmas was what we came to understand as walkie-talkies. They were usually small, battery-operated devices that allowed two people to communicate with each other when they were not even in the same space. The thing that made them so special was the fact that they closed a gap. For instance, I can remember one year in particular that my neighbor was blessed to receive walkie-talkies, so I learned vital communication principles. Although we did not live in the same house, we could speak to each other late at night without our parents being aware. What a marvelous toy. We had our own special codes of communication, just the two of us. It closed a communication gap between our homes and gave us the ability to share and communicate more easily. It opened up new possibilities, just as proper communication principles will do when applied in our marriage. These principles will release us into new levels of sharing and expressing our concerns and desires.

Use the Button

We quickly learned something about our walkie-talkies. When we would talk, at first, the communication was broken and hard to hear. We both were trying to talk at the same time. We found that the devices only worked when we did not attempt to talk at the same time. If I pushed my button, spoke, and then released my button, giving him an opportunity to speak, they worked perfectly. Can I share this communication principle with you? Whenever both people are trying to talk at the same time, it will never be clear. Something will always be missed. Only when the respect of rhythm is provided will communication become crystal clear. Learning how to listen to the other person and not short-circuit their words can insure that communication flows.

Sound always operates in waves, and therefore a principle of communication is observing and honoring the wave of communication. Learn to listen and respond. Also, when responding, only respond to the statement as received. Understanding how to properly use the button can be remembered by three simple components of communication: expressing, listening, and responding. All communication falls into one of these three categories. We should always be sensitive to which of these three areas we are using and are in need of communicating from at any given time. They represent three distinct areas and instruments of good communication. We are expressing ourselves, listening to others, or responding to what has been shared. If these three areas are to operate in godly order, there must be new levels of strategic sensitivity about operating the buttons that release each of them correctly.

Replace the Batteries

Once again, can I draw your attention to the childhood toys? When my friend and I had walkie-talkies and one of us did not remain sensitive to the batteries, communication could become broken. While it was still capable of sending and receiving signals, if the battery strength was weak, the signal would also be weak. Static would make hearing difficult. We never talk about spirituality in relation to communication, but it is very important. Replacing the battery in the toy is symbolic of keeping our devotional life strong as a believer. When we properly manage our relationship with Christ, our spirits become open and sensitive when communicating with each other. Our spiritual batteries must be strong to ensure strong signal reception and transmission.

Interference

Since walkie-talkies transmit signals between the two devices, if and when anything is allowed to stand either in between them or too close to them, communication is affected. For instance, if my friend and I stood close to the television, the signal from the television would interfere with the signal of the communication device and cause static. Or, let's say one of us walked around the back of the house. The house would break the signal because it would not bend around the corner. The principle is true about communication in our marriages. We must guard our communication from interference. Allowing people outside of our marriage to become too close can make communication with our spouses a problem. As well, allowing someone to stand between you and your spouse can produce such a level of static that communication can be drastically altered. Can I suggest that many times we simply have too many confidants and mentors from whom we seek advice? We cannot run to in-laws and family and allow them to become a source of static and broken communication. By routinely checking for static, we can be confident that communication will always be open and strong.

Watch the Frequency

Most walkie-talkies come with the ability to adjust the frequency or channel in which you desire to communicate. This enables you to fine-tune the communication sequencing and prevent other people from hearing what you say. Wow! Can you imagine what type of communication success we could have in our marriages if we regularly checked to see if we were on the same frequency? In fact, if our frequency is checked regularly, we can prevent other people from listening to our conversation. The principle of frequency is based upon examining when we should communicate and with whom we are released to communicate with outside of our marriage. When a couple decides with whom they are allowed to share and communicate outside of their relationship, they maintain a frequency of confidentiality that ensures the receiving of sound advice, guidance, and counsel. You cannot talk to everyone. Please note that not everyone does qualifies to give advice. Designating the advice-givers is a proven process for keeping your frequency of communication clear, accessible, and strong.

The On-Off Switch

I need to remind you that walkie-talkies only work when turned on. I know this sounds very simple, but when the other person's walkie-talkie is turned off, they cannot hear you. Before you stop reading because that is so simple, hear me out. I am simply stating a basic truth that many times is overlooked and taken for granted. Are you not aware that sometimes the simplest things trip us up? Remember that Israel defeated Jericho but lost to Ai, the smallest city in the region. Small things can have a big impact. Before communication can take place, both instruments of communication must be operational, or turned on.

What does it mean to turn on the device? Make sure that you position yourself to listen. When one person is turned off, you waste your time communicating. For instance, when a man first comes home, he wants to simply chill for a moment, unwind, relax, and regroup. This time might only be thirty minutes, but most men need that time. Women should know that if you start communicating the moment he comes home, usually his receiver will be in the off position. Certain times of the month or week can be very difficult opportunities for talking. The establishment of a planned time to talk is important. Why talk at ineffective times? Both husband and wife need to be open and ready to communicate. Establishing a preplanned time for communication is still only as effective as our commitment to staying on task with the plan. It requires planning and commitment but will yield tremendous rewards in the communication process.

Time Versus Distance

Finally, I can remember that sometimes when we talked on the walkie-talkies, it would take some time for the communication to actually reach the other device. This was because there was a long distance between the two devices. It was kind of like a delayed reaction. If we were not sensitive to the distance, communication would become difficult or some of the words would be missed. Can I explain this principle from the perspective of a man and a woman? When major decisions are being made, men need extended time to think. The place that they go to think is what we call "the cave." It can be the gym, the garage, or even the store, but they need that time alone. Men need delayed time in the cave, sometimes, during the communication process. Remember earlier when we talked about the difference between a man and a woman, we shared that men do not process on the spot. Whenever two people are communicating and there is some distance between their positions, there could very well be some delay in receiving the signal. Be aware that it could possibly take some time for the other person to understand what is being shared. Patience many times can make communication easier. Share your perspective and then wait for a response. Do not push or place time ultimatums or limits on the communication process.

Good communication cannot be rushed. The delay is not a bad sign. The delay is simply indicative of the process. Invest the time, operate with patience, respect the delay, and do not give opportunity for Satan to take advantage of the down time. While waiting for a spouse to respond, take advantage of the delay by spending time praying and seeking the direction of God.

Finally, the toy that I have used as an illustration is called, once again, a walkie-talkie. The very name of the toy implies that it is designed to be used while we are moving. Moving and speaking is the posture of righteousness. As believers, God declares that our steps are ordered by Him. "Steps" is meant to refer to movement. We are supposed to be going somewhere. I have discovered that when both husband and wife are moving, growing, and developing, communication is more effective. However, we must be moving in the same direction. This movement is a vital component of the unit required to communicate. When we are moving together, communication moves to greater depths as well. If we are not careful to monitor our movement, we will find that we have allowed too much distance between us and that communication is affected. We must do communication maintenance. Check the batteries, watch the frequency, turn on the device, operate the buttons correctly—and God will do the rest!

The Mind of Communication

My beautiful wife and I are totally different. She is left-brained and I am right-brained. Left-brained people usually communicate and process sequentially, cognitively, methodically, and with little external emotion. Right-brained people usually process and communicate spontaneously, imaginatively, with gray areas, and tend to be externally, emotionally driven. In most marital relationships, one person is right-brained and one person is left-brained. Stopping to survey and understand how your spouse processes can make it much easier to establish a foundation and benchmark for communicating based upon how they process.

Because I am a right-brained person, I do not usually plan anything, while my wife is always planning. Vacations are planned, her week is planned, and the menu is planned. When we go on vacation, she desires to have a family meeting and decide what attractions we will visit and how we will spend the duration of the vacation. It becomes difficult to communicate that with me, because I just want to wake up, go driving, and see what the area has to offer. How does she communicate her desire with me? Visuals! Brochures! My wife will gather all of the pamphlets that she can and show me where she desires the family to visit during the week. This process works better for me than anything else. It allows me to see what she is attempting to communicate. Because of how I process, she has discovered how to communicate with a clear understanding of my perspectives and mental abilities. Remember that opposites attract. God wired us. We are called to be responsible to understand our differences and to allow our differences to become our greatest asset for communication.

Handling Disagreements

Time and words are not redeemable and should be used with great concern and compassion. Many times in the heat of a disagreement, we say things that we regret and cannot take back. The relationship may be damaged. It may take a great deal of time for the relationship to heal. There are some lessons we can employ in order to maintain a civil respect for our spouse when we find ourselves in disagreement. Maintaining a positive outlook and perspective is always helpful. Too often we engage in disagreements with the desire to win. Men, especially, feel the need to win when sharing their perspective in the midst of disagreements and arguing. If we begin to approach times of disagreement as opportunities to fix something broken in the relationship rather than as an opportunity for a victory, it forces the couple to operate in an atmosphere of compromise. When disagreements take place, if each spouse will approach the moment with a positive outlook and a willingness to entertain the possibility that he or she is to blame, it can further produce an openness that allows for personal expression without personal offense.

Remember, blame has to be taken. It can never be given. When we are willing to accept blame, it prevents us from being closed-minded and releases us to be open to the perspectives of others. Upon hearing the perspective of others, it might be clear that the situation was not as it was originally thought to have been. It is also very helpful during the discussion and time of disagreement to be willing to take the high road of apology. Apologizing can be one of the most difficult moments in the life of any couple. Admitting that you are wrong does not always come easy and can be hard to swallow. Apologizing is not always the result of intentional pain or wrong action. We are responsible to apologize, even when the pain we have inflicted was not intentional. When we cause other people pain and they acknowledge the behavior that caused the pain, they place a responsibility on us to make it right. Feelings are reality. If a person has been hurt, it does not matter if there was intention to hurt. Sincerely apologize and display behavior that is genuine in your attempt to move beyond the pain of the encounter.

When we find ourselves in the midst of a disagreement, we should be committed to expressing our hurt and pain and not our emotions and hostility. Address the behavior, not the trauma. Express instead how the behavior made you feel, without displaying behavior based upon the feeling. We do this by making direct statements and not absolute statements. Absolute statements are too vague and do not always apply. Absolute statements are those such as, "You always do that," or "You never do this." Every situation should be considered in its own context. When we use absolute statements, we incorporate events and circumstances that should not be invited into the current situation.

While avoiding absolute statements, we should remain solution centered. Bringing up problems without solutions is not helpful. If we are honestly working toward solutions and not personal victory, then we should be willing to hear and share prospective solutions. Remember, we communicate based upon circumstances and dialogue, with the desire of fixing what is broken. One of the areas in which we must remain sensitive is when we seek counsel outside of our marriage. Many times, in order to find solutions and remain open-minded we need someone who is on the outside and can speak clearly to the situation with unbiased, godly wisdom. Not everyone is qualified to serve as your counsel. Only those who have proven track records should be sought out for guidance. Proven confidants who can speak truth without compromise, who are led by God, and who desire to genuinely see your marriage improve qualify to counsel. Seeking counsel from unqualified individuals can many times create more trouble than improvement.

Because we can become so emotionally driven during a disagreement, pushing us to think irrationally, we must always be willing to examine ourselves, our perspectives, and our motives. Ask yourself these questions: Am I jumping to a conclusion? Am I thinking clearly? Am I overreacting? These are healthy questions to ask. Not only should we ask questions of ourselves, but we must ask the question, When is a good time to communicate? The selection of a time in which the level of stress is reduced and the environment is more conducive to sound communication is imperative. Talking at the wrong time can cause emotional overload and take things from bad to worse. Choose a time when reflection and processing has opened our minds and spirits to the possibilities of reaching compromise. Proverbs 15:1 teaches us to respond with soft answers. It also states that harsh words can cause even more strife. Rehearsing how something sounds before saying it is helpful. Putting yourself in your spouse's position can also cause you to hear from their perspective. Many times things sound different when we hear them from the vantage point of others. While we know that Satan desires to divide us, we do not have to give entry to his schemes.

Finally, one of the greatest concepts for handling and preventing disagreements is to establish rules and guidelines and set operational boundaries. For example, my wife and I have established that when we disagree about extended family moments, we will make ourselves the "heavy" in relation to each side of the family. Let me explain. If my family wants us to come over for dinner and we decide we cannot attend, I communicate to my family and share that I decided we could not make it tonight. I never allow my wife to be the bad guy when it is my side of the family, and she does not put me in the position of having to be the bad guy when it is her side of the family. Establishing this simple rule has prevented Satan from bringing division in the ranks of our extended family. Remember, your parents will not remain angry with you but will potentially hold a grudge against your spouse for years. Think about areas, such as dealing with in-laws, in which you can be proactive by developing rules of engagement that will produce harmony, strength, and peace in your relationship. Too many times we wait until we have to be reactive, which forces us to think during emotionally unstable times, causing unnecessary pain and hardship.

Chapter 13

The Trust Factor

I CAN STILL SMELL THE fried chicken cooking on the stove. I was on top of the world. Good job, new wife, new son, new ministry, and a great home. Life was good! As the American dream goes, I had arrived. What I did not know was that Satan was busy behind the scenes planning an attack on my new relationship with Valerie. It was a bright, sunny day, so I decided to wash my wife's car while she finished preparing dinner. That sunny Saturday evening I learned my first and greatest lesson about trust. When I opened the trunk to her car, I found a pair of men's bedroom slippers. They were new leather slippers with fur inside. I immediately checked the size, because maybe my new wife was planning to surprise me with a gift. Size 11. Size 11— I wore size 9! Who did these shoes belong to? Where did they come from? Was my new wife cheating on me? "Of course she is," the little devil on my shoulder informed me. I could not believe this, but confrontation was the only way to handle this moment. I would not be mistreated. She needed to explain. I angrily rushed into the kitchen, slammed the shoes on the counter, and demanded an answer to my inquiry. As she continued to cook, she peacefully responded, "I don't know who they belong to." Did she think I was that dumb or naïve? Being the right-brained, emotional person that I am, I began to get louder and louder until finally she broke. Her crying was proof that she was, indeed, guilty. I wanted to know, Where does he live? Do I know him? Even through her tears, she continued to insist that there was no man. I don't recall now if I was mad because it appeared that she had a relationship with another man or because he was bigger than me and had nicer bedroom slippers.

About two weeks later, after many nights of silence and my sleeping on the sofa, she reminded me that my nephew had spent the night at our home two weeks earlier. Before taking him home we had placed his clothing in the trunk of the car. She suggested that the slippers were his. Still not willing to believe her, I called my sister-in-law to inquire about my nephew's bedroom slippers. You guessed it. They had been missing for two weeks. He left them at my house.

At that point I felt terrible. I had allowed Satan to play me. I had acted like a fool. I never had reason to suspect my wife of being unfaithful. How stupid could I be? How would I make up for it? Trust is a precious commodity in a marriage. More precious than gold, it is to be valued, honored, and respected. Trust cannot be given—it must be earned.

Just as I allowed Satan to play me, please know that mistrust is the door that Satan walks through many times in our marriages. All he really needs is to recognize that the door is unlocked, and he will do the rest. I have learned that we can and must become proactive in protecting the trust in our marriages. While it takes work, building trust is possible when we commit to behavior that prevents Satan from getting any foothold in our minds that can produce thoughts that erode the level of healthy trust.

Trustproof Your Marriage

Trust is the result of a healthy environment and continued hard work. Some men have been trained and conditioned to think that real men do not do things like check-in at home. But real men do understand that Satan wants their marital relationship at any cost, and they are committed to working hard to preserve the integrity of their relationship.

My wife and I developed several strategies that have kept the spirit of trust alive and strong in our relationship. First, we call each other often, when leaving the office or leaving appointments, for example. This keeps Satan from stealing our time or giving the appearance of time spent with others. We do not have time for affairs, but that does not stop Satan from planting the thoughts of time and opportunity in your mind. Being open with your time can really let the air out of the balloon of the adversary. We both keep each other's schedule. She knows my schedule, and I know her schedule.

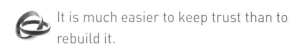 It is much easier to keep trust than to rebuild it.

Another simple thing that we do is to trade cell phones. I heard the response, "Wow!" I am amazed at how many married couples are not open to trading cell phones. What do you have to hide? Trust is too important to allow Satan opportunity to attack. Please know that Satan is attacking anyway. I do not have to give him the instruments to use. I want to make it as difficult as possible to attack my marriage; perhaps then he will move on to much easier relationships elsewhere. Trading cell phones, having a joint cell phone account, and not locking your phone are quick, easy, relatively painless ways to build trust in a marriage. I still remember the Sunday that I suggested trading cell phones during my sermon. I heard later that after church the men's restroom was full of men deleting numbers from their cell phones.

Another way that we have continued to trustproof our

marriage is by being sensitive to spending time in questionable places. Environment is important. I observe many couples that work out at fitness locations without their spouses. Our church provides a fitness and weight program to give believers an opportunity to exercise in an environment that is more suited to maintaining trust in relationships. I often take my son with me on the road as a witness of my behavior and environment. It prevents Satan from planting seeds of thoughts in the mind of my wife and provides me with an accountability partner. Traveling with an accountability partner is a great resource. Being around people who will not tolerate or allow behavior that is not acceptable can take the pressure off of any relationship. Remember, most affairs begin spontaneously. They are the result of bad thinking and environment.

Many couples have separate financial and billing vehicles as well. For instance, separate banks and billing addresses. Some couples even have post office box addresses that their spouses do not know about. Many times people use their businesses as covers for questionable types of behavior. While it is understandable that business and personal transactions need to be separate, there must be an openness that allows for a level of comfort and confidence between spouses. If I cannot trust my spouse with access to my financial information, then there are much deeper concerns in our relationship. While we understand that there can be extenuating circumstances such as substance abuse concerns or spending addictions that have impact on disclosure and usage, providing some form of information transfer is vital in building and maintaining trust.

If Satan is looking for any area of entrance, it can be through finances. My wife takes care of all of our finances. She pays the bills, banks the money, and determines the savings. She pays our tithes and is fully responsible for the financial movement of our family. Satan often reminds me of how little I know about our household finances. He asks questions like, "Where is the money going?" or, "Is she hiding money for her benefit only?" Because of the sensitivity of my wife, she never hides the checkbook. I have full access to it at all times. I can look at the checks she has written at any time. In fact, when she makes a transfer or pays an unusually large bill, such as property tax, she is careful to write it in the check register for my clarity. As well, she will communicate with me when those tight moments exist. She keeps me informed, reducing the ability of Satan to deal with my mind and impact my level of trust for her.

Whenever someone of the opposite sex writes me a letter or e-mail that I think has crossed the line, I share it with my wife. Many times when I am responding to the e-mail or letter of a female, I seek Valerie's advice and input about what to say and how to say it.

God has allowed us to develop an unusual sensitivity to maintaining healthy trust in our relationship. Developing sensitivity for dealing with people of the opposite sex is vital in maintaining healthy levels of trust. As stated earlier, trust is too valuable to not deserve constant evaluation and refining. When I call the home of a married woman, I ask to speak with her husband. This builds respect and empowers the trust in my marriage. I never counsel a woman without having staff present in the vicinity. This develops even healthier levels of trust. Trust is the result of planned activity and processes.

Rebuilding Trust

With much hard work, time, genuine effort, and commitment, trust can be restored. I have discovered that it can take as long or longer to rebuild trust to the point at which it was breached as it did to build trust in the first place. For instance, after twelve years of trust, one moment can erase and erode the level of trust to the point that it might take twelve years to fully recover. I realize that this sounds extreme, but trust is not easily regained. It takes time to build—but can take only a moment to lose.

Every relationship is different and therefore should not be compared or measured by other relationship models. Since every relationship is different, the weak points or areas of concern are different. Couples should take time to discuss satanic entry points in their relationship during the foundational years of the relationship. Certain careers have the potential to make trust issues loom larger than others. Careers with a lot of downtime and high pay, for instance, require greater sensitivity than perhaps a career working from the home. Careers involving extended travel, especially with people of the opposite sex, require attention as well.

The rebuilding of trust will usually require several points of consideration. First, it must be remembered that the person who has breached the trust is at the full obligation and mercy of the wounded spouse. In other words, when trust is broken, it becomes the responsibility of the trust-breaking spouse to accept the conditions determined by the victimized spouse as a process of rebuilding trust. This can be difficult because, I have noticed, many times we mistake forgiveness with the plan for restoration. Just because grace has abounded and the couple has moved into a process of healing does not mean the trust-breaking spouse is released from the steps and process needed by the hurting spouse, who is challenged to trust again. I also think that it is always healthy to have, as a part of the established process of restoration, a person who can assist the couple in developing a fair yet structured, impartial process.

Many times when we are hurting, it becomes difficult to

remain open-minded when establishing the steps of restoration. Someone who is impartial and not ruled by their emotions can bring structure and experience to a couple desiring to move past broken trust and into a restored and healthy relationship. Any plan of restoration should also include measureable expectations and continued monitoring and counseling. One of the things that any couple should realize is that they need external assistance in moving past the breach of trust. It takes time, counseling, planning, and measured monitoring to provide the best opportunity possible for full relationship restoration and reestablishment of trust.

Finally, I have learned that putting yourself in your spouse's position when making decisions can be helpful in establishing deeper trust. I try to always remain conscious of how any moment would look to me if my wife were engaging in the behavior that I am engaging in. If I think that I would not understand or appreciate the action or activity, then that should serve as a signal to me that the behavior should be altered. Always try to think how it looks to others, and when you feel any concern, chances are the behavior is not acceptable.

We have also trained ourselves to be sensitive to new behavior patterns. A change in perfume or cologne or a sudden desire to exercise can all be used by Satan to plant seeds of division, confusion, and suspicion. Our greatest desire should be to earn the confidence of our spouse and confirm that confidence with assured behavior. This makes it extremely difficult for Satan to even suggest impropriety or distrust.

Chapter 14

Unpacking Our "Baggage"

Wʜᴇɴ ᴡᴇ ɢᴇᴛ ᴍᴀʀʀɪᴇᴅ, we are not just marrying a person but all of their experiences, their culture, their family, and their way of thinking. All of these components comprise what I call "baggage." *Baggage* is not a bad word. We all have baggage. Because we are all human and no one is perfect, we all bring baggage into our relationships. While some may have more "bags" than others, no one is without the stress and struggles of life that produce those things that we are not proud of but have to live with. To the extent that we learn to acknowledge our own baggage and understand how to deal with it, life can become much easier to navigate and handle. I believe our baggage falls into three major categories that are the sum total of all baggage. We have sociological baggage, which includes our emotional and psychological baggage; geographical baggage; and spiritual baggage. While I am sure we could agree that there are many other categories that could be included, I believe these to be the big three.

Sociological Baggage

As hard as this might be to believe, when I first got married almost twenty years ago, my wife, Valerie, and I argued over simple things, such as drinking orange juice. I would be cutting the grass, come inside from the heat outside, and pour a tall glass of orange juice. It would drive her crazy. She would reply, "Orange juice is a breakfast drink. You should drink water." For the first two years, we did not understand why such simple things evolved into big arguments. Then one day it all made sense. We were reared totally different sociologically. She had been reared in a home with both parents. Her stay-at-home mother would fix breakfast, and the family ate together. Orange juice was considered a breakfast drink. In my single-parent home, orange juice was a beverage to be consumed whenever it was available. It might not always be available. Slowly but surely, we began to understand each other better. We had been reared totally differently. Her two-parent household had conditioned her to think differently than my one-parent household. As we continued to learn, we noticed other differences. Dinner was one of those differences. I ate dinner when I was hungry, and she ate dinner at a set time. I ate in front of the television, and she always wanted to eat at the dinner table. We were different because of how we had been reared. She wanted to process the day during dinner. I simply wanted to eat. While we would soon learn that neither she nor I was better than the other, we did discover that we were very different. We had been raised in the same area but with different perspectives. While our values were the same, our rearing was not. Now, twenty years later, I have learned that there are many sociological implications in our rearing that have impact on our ability to understand our spouses.

Birth order can be important. Firstborn children with siblings can be bossy and are almost always born leaders. Middle children can many times have self-esteem issues and feel like they have to demand attention. Children that are the babies of the family are sometimes conditioned to have expectations of provision, service, and comfort. They many times expect someone else to take care of them due to their being raised with older siblings.

I am the baby of my family, and although I have a brother and a sister, we were not reared together. I was actually reared in an only child environment. People reared as the only child in a home can sometimes be selfish. I can say this because I know I can be selfish by nature. My wife, on the other hand, has an older sister who was reared in the home with her. This is another difference. My wife was given her older sister's leftover dresses. I was an only child who always got everything new.

One of our greatest differences was always toy buying at Christmas. As an only child, Christmas was major for me; there were always lots of toys. As the youngest child in a single-income family, Christmas was not about toys for my wife but about family. I always want to buy a lot at Christmas time. My wife, on the other hand, wants to share the experience and not allow it to be overshadowed with toys.

Not only is our birth order important to understand, but our parental relationships and dynamics as well. My wife is the youngest of two girls in her family. She is, in fact, the "son" that my father-in-law never had. She plays sports, watches sports, and many times, thinks like a man. She is very competitive. As I stated earlier, I was raised by a single mother. When Valerie and I first got married, we had different perspectives on making the bed. Valerie wants the bed made every morning before we leave the home. As a child, my mother left before I did to go to work, so I never made my bed in the morning. I just made sure it was made before she got home from work. I did not wash clothes as a boy or cook or clean (other than my room). When I got married, I had not been conditioned to make the bed every morning, wash clothes, or cook. This always led to arguments in my marriage.

Another area of our thinking impacted by our childhood is money management. We learn how to manage money through our rearing. My mother grew up poor in North Carolina. She made up in her mind that as an adult, she would have the finest things in life, even if she could not afford them. My wife once again was reared totally differently. Her father was a saver. In fact, he retired when his daughter was still in college. A credit card was for emergencies in the home of my wife. In my house as a child, a credit card was as good as cash. If it had an available limit, charge it! When my mother died, she was in debt up to her eyeballs. When my father-in-law died, he was debt free. We were an argument waiting to happen! I wanted to spend; she wanted to save. I had no problem with bill collectors calling my house. My wife hated for bills to be behind. What a struggle life was until we really began to understand how we had been reared and that ultimately the only true path of stewardship was in the Bible, not in our childhood homes.

As a part of my growth, we went through a period in which I was not allowed to have a credit card because I could not control my spending. I had been reared to spend money. While I have come a long way, I only began to make progress when I acknowledged that my habits came from my rearing examples.

I have also found that the gender in single-parent households is important to study. Let me explain. For a female raised by a single mom, it may be harder to accept the leadership of a husband. This is not because she does not want to but because she has not seen male leadership in the home. My mother was very strong and manipulative. Before I got married, I had determined that no woman would ever tell me what to do with my finances. Because of how I had been reared by my single mother, it became very hard to yield the financial leadership to my wife. I had watched my mother take my paycheck and gamble, so I was determined to not allow any woman to operate in that way in my life again. It almost cost my family its financial stability because I would not yield to the most qualified person in our home—my wife, Valerie—to handle our finances.

Can I share another unseen cultural area that can provide baggage? Careers can have great impact on how we think and respond. Careers that require and demand respect, such as police officers or lawyers, might make it hard to handle moments in the home where respect can appear to be breached. As one example, a lawyer must leave the courtroom at work when they get home. In discussions, they must keep in mind that they are not cross-examining their spouse; they are communicating. Almost every career choice has an impact on our day-to-day lives and should be considered when processing our behavior and patterns of thinking.

Whether we are the oldest child or youngest child, middle child or firstborn, single parent or traditional family, any of these components impact our thinking and processing. We must understand these components in order to understand ourselves. These are only a few of the areas that we must understand in order to develop a stronger relationship in marriage.

There are many other areas that can and should be explored. I have simply attempted to challenge your thinking. Personal study can only serve to increase the insight that can be found with greater self-understanding. I challenge all couples to use this insight to develop your own cultured paradigms in order to find a common ground of understanding about yourself and your spouse. Baggage, when defined and understood, can become an asset. But, baggage left packed and unprocessed can prove to be detrimental to a healthy relationship.

Geographical Baggage

I have never heard of anyone exploring geographical baggage, but it has a real and powerful impact on our marriages. Where we were reared—big city, small town, townhouse, apartment, single-family house, or farmhouse—can affect our thinking. Exploring our geographical baggage can help explain why we are who we are. I was raised in Portsmouth, Virginia. Valerie was raised in Chesapeake, Virginia. Although they are sister cities, when we were young they were and remain different. Chesapeake does not have a downtown area. The city of Chesapeake is really quite suburban. For the most part, it is new and middle class. The city itself is less than forty years old. Schools are relatively new, and the race demographic is 80 percent white and 20 percent African American. My hometown, Portsmouth, is much older, a little more urban, and the race demographics are almost the opposite of Chesapeake. Crime in Portsmouth is higher than in Chesapeake. As a young adult, I had cars stolen, saw houses broken into, and witnessed friends who were killed in shoot-outs. My wife experienced none of those types of things. We had a security officer in our school. She cannot imagine that.

This has conditioned how we think and operate in life. She never locks the car doors. I lock the doors to the car, even in the garage. I have serious trust issues. "Everyone is trying to con you," is how I think. My wife is more trusting than I am and will give everyone the benefit of the doubt. She takes everyone at face value. I tend to trust no one at first, and my trust is hard to earn. This can even impact our priorities. I grew up with many friends from the projects. In Chesapeake, even the projects were single-family homes. I placed greater value on cars than homes when I first got married. The house could be falling apart, but the car would be clean and new. My wife places more value on the home and can drive the same car for fifteen years.

I have also seen the impact of geographical baggage in the marriages of many who I counsel. Big city people do not usually speak to everyone they pass, but small town people do. Small town people tend to move at a much slower pace than large city people. Our priorities can be very different. Small town people drive, and large city people take the taxis or the subway. Can I share something funny with you? My daughter is a student at North Carolina A&T University. She does not have a car on campus. It did not dawn on me that she had never ridden in a taxi until she went away to school. Her first taxi ride was a real education for her because it was a totally new experience. Because she was reared in a city with very little public transportation, she has had to learn how to catch the bus and to use a taxi for transportation.

Another way in which geographical baggage can impact our lives is through travel and life experiences. My wife has lived in Washington, DC, and has traveled the world. I have never lived anywhere other than Hampton Roads. We currently live twenty miles from where I was born. Her experience of living in a large metropolitan area for several years has impacted how she thinks. She brings experiences to our marriage because of that season in her life. The more I study our lives, the more qualified I become to understand how to use our baggage for our benefit. Remember, baggage is only bad when not acknowledged or when not understood.

Spiritual Baggage

While we often talk about social and emotional baggage that we bring into our marriages, it can be difficult to talk about our spiritual baggage. I have very rarely, if ever, heard anyone mention the religious baggage we carry. All of us have religious baggage, even those who are not Christians or religious. Even an atheist has religious beliefs. They believe that God does not exist. These beliefs sometimes can become problems in our marital relationships. They may create situations and dilemmas that must be understood and dealt with.

Sometimes these differences are denominationally driven: what we believe about the Word of God, and what it means to be a follower of Christ; how we respond to women; what we think about church; what our responsibilities are to church through service and giving. I believe that many believers are not equally yoked. Although this term originally referred to a union between a believer and a non-believer, I believe it can also apply to those who do not think the same way about their faith. When we have blatantly different religious perspectives, we can have a great deal of difficulty in reaching common spiritual ground. Some denominations have very archaic perspectives on the role of women in the home and in the church. Others are very liberal in social roles, while still others are very conservative. Some might embrace different levels of evangelism and doctrine. Whatever the denomination, it shapes our thinking. In fact, many denominational hang-ups can cause separation in families and how they treat and respond to each other. This concern is actually beyond just the Christian faith. Other religious movements actually have standards preventing marrying someone outside of their faith.

How to spend Sunday is interesting denominational baggage. I have had opportunities to share with couples who would argue over how their Sundays should be spent. One spouse desires to go to church and then spend the remainder of the day with family activity. They desire to go to the beach or the amusement park. The other spouse feels as though Sunday is a day for church from morning worship until afternoon training or afternoon worship. As simple as this may sound, it posed great problems in their relationships. Only after recognizing that neither of them was right but that they both needed to recognize their baggage was I able to help them. Let me explain. The spouse who only wanted to go to morning worship was not raised in church as a child, so going to church at all was a great improvement in his or her spiritual walk. Added to this was the value placed on spending time with family. The other spouse grew up in a ministry home, and every Sunday they went to worship, then over to grandmother's house for dinner and back to church for additional church moments. When the couple began to understand why they thought differently, they were able to open themselves up for compromise. Remember, when it comes to the marriage relationship, it is not only about right and wrong but also the health, success, and unity in the relationship.

I have discovered how religious baggage can impact our relationships in other areas as well. How should we dress, and how should we handle domestic responsibilities? Who should cook? Should we cook on Sunday or on Saturday evening? Other questions might be: Should we go to the movies on Sunday? Can we listen to secular music? How about dancing? Is it allowed? What kind of clothing can we wear? Is makeup allowed? Is makeup sin? Can women wear pants? I know you are saying, "Come on, Pastor!" But please, let me remind you that we are conditioned for many years before we get married, and we bring all those years of conditioning into our relationships. It becomes extremely hard to erase years of reinforcement. I can remember dealing with couples in which the wife always wanted to go out and eat on Sunday and the husband felt that the wife was to prepare a meal for the whole family on Sunday. What a problem! You guessed it. Spiritual baggage. He was raised to have family dinner every Sunday after church. She was not raised in church, and that, coupled with her big-city hometown, had conditioned her to think differently than he thought. No one was right, and no one was wrong. They were different in their thinking resulting from how they were raised.

Suitcases, briefcases, overnight bags, or stand-up bags—whatever your baggage looks like—we all have bags. When we unzip them, open them up, and begin to understand why we have packed what is inside, marriage can be awesome! However, it takes work and honest, emotional interrogation to take this step.

Allow the Holy Spirit to assist you in sorting through your baggage, and plan exercises with your spouse to accomplish this task. Watch God open your relationship to new possibilities of understanding. Please God through your marriage, and become a great witness to the kingdom. Help others to reconcile their actions, and bring clarity to how they, too, have been conditioned to think.

Chapter 15

Intimacy and Sexuality

ONE OF THE REASONS that I felt inspired to write this book was because the body of Christ is sometimes reluctant to deal with real issues. We need something that can be relevant and real. When we talk about sexuality, many times we water it down and do not give the Holy Spirit the opportunity to manifest change through revelation. Let's be real! Let's talk about real issues. We have some serious problems in our marital society: men on the down low, women exploring new gender-bending options, pornography addictions and child molestation are rampant. Our young people are confused and seeking answers to questions that we want to ignore. Teen pregnancy is at an all-time high. And as for the ages of the people having babies—well, *babies* are having babies. We need to talk, so let's talk!

The Purpose of Sex

Much of our society's sexual dysfunction is grounded in the fact that many of us have never properly understood why God created sex in the first place. Sex is a gift from God, designed to accomplish at least four things: procreation, communication, information, and recreation.

Whenever believers are asked why sex exists, they will almost always reply, "Procreation." Although this is perhaps the main reason for sex, it is not the only reason. Sex is indeed the process and vehicle that God utilizes to give mankind the privilege and opportunity to share in the creation of life. Life is a creation based upon the union of man and woman. I must remind us of something. If sex is created to give and manifest life, then it points us to a truth: any relationship that cannot have an opportunity to produce life cannot be ordered by God. Only when a man and a woman come together can life be produced—Adam and Eve, not Adam and Steve. Just a thought to be pondered!

The second reason for sex and intimacy is communication. Over nineteen years of pastoring, I have observed that marriages with weak communication also many times tend to be marriages with issues in their intimate life. I am sure you will agree that intimacy breeds communication. It can be hard to be physically together and not talk. Sexual relationships can force two people to communicate. Whether they are sharing feelings of pleasure, desires, expectations, or gratefulness, communication is taking place. Communication, in fact, can be vital to satisfying sexual encounters. We are forced to share how we feel and what we need. Especially for men, sex can become the door through which they are allowed to understand themselves better.

Communication can also lead to a more efficient way to receive information. We can learn a lot about our loved one during the moments of intimacy. In fact, sex is supposed to be a classroom. When sharing sexual moments with our spouse, we enroll in a class and study the person with whom we share our intimate moments. We can learn more about our spouse in sexually intimate moments than perhaps in any other moment in life. We learn their emotions, needs, and desires. Sex should be a time of exploration, a moment in which we can step outside of our comfort zones and learn more about ourselves. We learn how to become unselfish. We learn how to express ourselves.

The first priority of sex is the satisfaction of
our spouse—not ourselves.

One of the greatest satisfactions in intimacy is being able
to satisfy the needs of your spouse. The first priority of sex is
the satisfaction of our spouse—not ourselves. Sexual intimacy
allows us to gather and receive information.

Finally, sexual moments allow us to enjoy one another. Consider
these moments as recreation. Once again, we never talk about
this in the body of Christ, but sex was created by God and created
to feel good. It should be pleasurable, enjoyable, and a celebra-
tion. In order for sex to be enjoyable, we must know our spouse.
Sex does not have to be sterile. We should not be intimidated to
express our desires to our spouse. Have fun! Role-play! Dress up!
Add spice to the relationship! God does not have a problem with
the enjoyment of life. In fact, God expects us to enjoy life. He
came that we might enjoy life (John 10:10). Sex is one of the vehicles He has given us to assist in making life pleasurable.

Love Banking

Love banking is a clinical concept for how we invest in our relationship with our spouse. While it can have emotional and
physical implications, love banking should be understood as a
principle that can have unprecedented effects on the health of
our marriages. Just as banks in our society are deposits of money,
the love bank is a depository for our emotions. In order to make
a bank withdrawal, you must have made a bank deposit. In short,
you cannot receive what you have not deposited. What are
deposits? Deposits are the statements we make, the compliments
we give, the gestures we share, and all of the things we can do to

make our spouse feel better about themselves, even something as simple as preparing that first cup of coffee in the morning. It could be preparing a favorite meal, sitting through a movie or play, watching a ballgame, riding in the cart while your husband plays golf, or the warm towel waiting at the shower door. These all represent deposits in the love bank.

Because life has so many distractions and demands on our time, we are usually operating on emotional credit and running an emotional deficit. Stopping to send flowers, taking a moment for a movie, saying a kind word, or acknowledging your wife's new dress ensures that we will keep a nice, high balance in our love bank accounts.

Sexual Fingerprints

Each of us has been conditioned by life to think the way that we do about our sexuality. Honestly, many people have had very little formal sexual education. Most of us learned what we know from friends and by trial and error. How we were raised and who we associated with play tremendous roles in developing what I call our "sexual fingerprint."

One of the most difficult realities to overcome is found to be the fact that many people grew up in a home where they did not witness any forms of affection being displayed. In generations past, parents were careful to keep their displays of affection private. I believe it is important to show affection in front of our children. I can remember one particular moment in the life of my family. One of the leaders in our church called my home one evening, only to be informed by my son that his parents were not available to talk at that time. My son proceeded to inform the gentleman that we were in the bedroom "knocking boots." (And yes, that is a euphemistic term for sexual intercourse.)

While I would not have desired that my son share our personal business with others (especially with that terminology!), I was excited to know that we had displayed positive behavior to help him to understand the relationship between a husband and wife. When my children were young they were trained to respect our closed bedroom door. We have never tried to hide the fact that their parents are in love with each other. We also thought it was very important to display affectionate behavior in front of them. Of course, we explained the inappropriateness of sharing this information with the caller, but it was refreshing to know we were training our children to understand and respect intimacy.

I believe that one of the reasons why we have so much sexual dysfunction in our society is because we do not properly educate our children. In fact, we start them out on a foundation that works counterproductively to understanding their sexuality. We teach children things about sexuality that are not true. We tell the story about storks and cabbage patches, so we begin their sexual education with a lie. In fact, most of us were taught early in life that sex was bad. How much more impact could we have when we teach them that sex is good and, in fact, a gift from God for married people?

I have never understood how we use negative statements, with the expectation of positive impact. "Just say no to drugs." Why don't we teach our young people to just say yes to life? Saying yes has a positive impact. Modeling behavior in front of our children can be a way of positively reinforcing and teaching proper appreciation for intimacy with our loved ones. Too many young people have never seen their parents express their feelings of love. Many young people, in fact, have never heard their parents say, "I love you." When we fail to model intimacy, we leave it up to the world to teach and display affection. This can lead to unrealistic emotional expectations.

Sexual Retraining

Since many people have learned how to embrace their sexuality from the world, many need to be retrained in how to respond to their spouse. Have you ever noticed how love scenes are played out on television and in the media? These scenes establish unrealistic processes in which we measure our sexual effectiveness. Television corrupts how intimacy is designed to operate in the life of a man and woman. In real life, we must invest time and energy in preparing for intimacy. As well, we must be aware of the correct buttons to push to enhance the sexual gratification of our spouse. In real life, one must be open to guidance. Because of the media, men have been taught that guidance from the wife is a statement that implies lack of masculinity, when, in fact, no one is a mind reader. How will we know the desires of our spouse if they are not shared and communicated?

Another place that the media has corrupted our sexual education is in the very act of intimacy. The media has shaped our minds to be warped about what is acceptable and is not acceptable. There are some activities that are not acceptable for believers. Because of pressure from the media and society, many times people feel a pressure to participate in activities that they are not comfortable practicing. However, we must examine our sexual fingerprints and determine how we think and why we think a certain way. Whether we had bad role models, no role models, or need to broaden our intimacy education, we can indeed become better stewards of one of the greatest God-given gifts to married people, the area of intimacy and sexuality.

Men must become open to instruction. Allow your wife to show you and communicate what she likes and desires. Wives must allow the baggage of upbringing to release their inhibitions. If we do these things, we will see the spark return to our marriages. The flame of our relationship will motivate and illuminate the relationships of others.

Establishing Sexual Boundaries

Whenever I am blessed to share in marriage conferences and other venues to teach and talk about marriage, I am asked questions about the acceptable activities for couples, especially Christian couples. For too long the church has turned a deaf ear to many of these questions. At times the answers to the questions were not grounded in biblical responsibility or they were masked in religious rhetoric. Subjects such as masturbation, oral sex, anal sex, and the use of toys and videos can no longer be ignored. Because I pastor a young congregation, I have been forced to deal with these issues.

As we dialogue about some of the most sensitive sexual issues that confront our society, I am aware that I enter territory in which I cannot win. The conservative believer will say I should not talk about such areas. The liberal will say that I am too dogmatic. I simply desire to allow God to speak through me so that men and women everywhere may be edified. As we tackle this subject, I am fully aware that much can be, and should be, said about sex and intimacy, but we will speak from a modern biblical vantage point.

We have often heard Hebrews 13:4 used to convey the notion that anything goes in the bedroom. When the Bible teaches us that the marriage bed is *undefiled*, it does not mean that any kind of sexual behavior by married people is acceptable to God but that what they do in their bedroom must be pure and sacred. There are those who teach that only a "traditional" sexual relationship is acceptable in marriage. Before going any further, let me that say that no spouse should be forced or pressured to do anything sexually that he or she does not feel comfortable doing.

But it needs to be remembered that many of the inhibitions felt between married people are grounded in bad teaching and lack of understanding about the original plan of God for our sexual lives. Remember, God created sex and made us sexual beings. He designed us to be attracted to the opposite sex. Sex is good. It must be understood and embraced properly. Where then should the boundaries be established?

 No spouse should be pressured to participate in sexual activity against his or her will.

Anything that engages us to operate contrary to the original plan of God I believe is wrong. For instance, the mouth was created to receive. In fact, the only time the mouth releases is when something is out of order. When we vomit, it is because something is wrong physically. The mouth is a receiver by creation. This is the basis of understanding that even in sexuality it is acceptable for the mouth to be involved for increased intimacy. Many of you will agree that because we have not attempted to find the heart and mind of God, we have fabricated stories and concepts with the intent of affecting behavior. How many young women were taught that oral sex was not lady-like? While oral sex might not be pleasant to everyone, it becomes difficult to find real biblical evidence against it.

The part of the body referred to as the anus was created to discharge. Anytime it is receiving something, it is out of order. It was created to release and not receive. Therefore, I believe that anal sex is not in line with the biblical desires of God. We can use the methodology of original intent to determine the actions and activities that are acceptable to God in all areas of our lives, not only sexual laws and practices. God planned and created man as he desired, so to operate contrary to the original intent of God is sin.

God also created sex to be between a man and a woman, a giver and a receiver. Men are givers, or transmitters, by creation. Women are receivers by creation. Anytime intimacy takes place between those who are not capable of giving and receiving, God is not pleased. Remember the chapter earlier on communication? Two receivers cannot communicate, nor can two transmitters communicate; someone must be receiving and someone must be transmitting. For example, the universe is established on the principle of divine exchange (giving and receiving). The ocean gives moisture to the atmosphere and then receives rain. The sun gives and receives. The flowers give and receive. This is a universal principle.

Sex is the coming together of a man and woman to make one flesh. That is a product of giving and receiving. While we do not judge same-sex couples, we must acknowledge that they do not operate in the original intent of God. God created us male and female and gave us sex as a gift to enjoy one another. To bring anything foreign into the relationship is out of order. When we use pornographic material, we establish unrealistic physical expectations and rob our spouse of the pleasure of learning how to sexually stimulate and satisfy. Masturbation can cause us to rob our spouse of the opportunity to receive guidance, direction, patience, and sensitivity while allowing us to satisfy ourselves.

 Nothing about intimacy is supposed to be founded in selfishness.

These external devices have a selfish foundation of self-gratification. Sex exists to provide the opportunity for spouses to meet the sexual needs of their partners, not themselves. When we satisfy ourselves, we establish a selfish baseline that can produce anxiety and tension in our marriage.

Pornographic videos portray images of sexuality that are not realistic and contribute to low sexual self-esteem in marriage. For example, think of foreplay as a great investment. For the wife, foreplay can be her husband's washing the dishes, cleaning the car, going to a movie, a nice dinner, or simply good conversation. Foreplay for the husband can be the unexpected phone call, the favorite red dress and the heels, or simply the smile that lets him know, "He's the man." Whatever form of foreplay works in your marriage, using mechanical devices as substitutes is not sexually healthy.

Rather than focus on what God does not allow within the sexual boundaries of marriage, I have found it much more beneficial to acknowledge those things that are acceptable. By accepting them we can open a whole new world of satisfaction, education, and sexual maturity that can produce new levels of intimacy, sexual fulfillment, and healthier marriages, while we remain faithful to our personal relationship with the Creator.

Chapter 16

Rearing Children

WHEN I WAS A child, the adults would always say that children were to be seen and not heard. This statement undergirds the fact that much of what we have been taught about rearing children needs to be reevaluated. Psalm 127:3 tells us children are gifts from God and parents are called to be stewards over the lives of their children. A trip to the mall on any day will display parental behavior that proves that we need to retool our parental thinking. Just a few days ago, I watched a young child throw a temper tantrum in the middle of the grocery store and watched as his mother counted to ten, waiting for him to change his behavior. Could it be that we have listened to too many people who have tainted our thinking to the point that our children are suffering from a lack of discipline and direction? Nintendo, Xbox, and PlayStation are the parents of today. I enjoy reading about great families in the history of our country and society and learning from their stories. I use their stories to shape much of my parental knowledge and standards for rearing my children. Parents must be eternal learners.

Parents are the premier role models for their children. In fact, parents are to be role models in every area of life. Parents show children how to make correct decisions. Parent's model their dependence on God and each other. Parents should be the chief example of godly devotion and spiritual development. Parents should also model personal discipline. Our children will only be as disciplined as they see us be. When I was a child, parents could drop their children off at church and go home. But today, we must model the discipline of worship before our children. We can no longer live by the motto "Do as I say, not as I do."

Children who observe godly parents grow up with a desire to serve God. Parents also are called to model determination. When parents quit, they teach their children to be quitters. I have always tried to make it hard for my children not to do their best or not see things through to the end by always completing my assignments. Even when it is difficult, I want my children to see me finish strong and with a sense of pride. Our children's decisions, dependence, devotion, discipline, determination, and overall development are inspired by the portrait that parents paint with their lifestyles. Did you know that in the Kennedy family, children are not allowed to have televisions in their bedrooms? What a great example they are to those of us who are rearing children via television and training them to work for money very early in their lives. I can remember my mother making me work for the senior neighbors and not allowing me to take money.

Much has changed in our world in respect to rearing children. It appears that if we do not change our style of rearing children, we run the risk of losing a whole generation. Even the terms that are used to refer to discipline have changed. When I was a child, discipline was referred to as punishment. It eventually became known as restriction, and still others refer to it as grounding. I love the language of the term *grounded*, because it really implies the goal of discipline. When I discipline my children, I should be attempting to make them more "grounded." Discipline is the process of training and correcting behavior. When people are properly grounded, they have established boundaries for their lives and make moral and ethical decisions based upon those boundaries. As parents, when we come to understand why God creates life in the first place, it makes the role of parenting clearer. Let's explore what must have been on the mind of God when He allowed humanity to participate in creating life.

 The family exists for the purpose of modeling the church and perpetually training believers.

The Purpose of Children

In generations past, we were taught not to ask questions of God or about God. But God does not have a problem with our questions and is not intimidated by them. Why did God allow humanity to participate in the process of creating life? Children exist for more than free labor to their parents. God does have a divine methodology behind the decision—to allow a man and a woman to assist in producing life.

Children are God's way of making sure that the kingdom of God continues to take territory on the Earth. In fact, the family exists for the purpose of modeling the church and perpetually training believers. The number one responsibility of parents is training their children. Each generation should actually be more intelligent and knowledgeable about the kingdom than the previous generation. Each generation should have more impact on the world for the kingdom than the previous generation. In short, parents are called to be educators—not friends, not teammates, but teachers. Our children should be enrolled as students in the University of Life, and our family households should be their classrooms.

The greatest achievement for parents is that their children graduate from the University of Life with honors. Children are

God's kingdom Social Security program. I tell people all the time that when you go to a church that has a small number of children, that is not a good sign. Children are proof that God has not given up on us. They declare with their presence that God is providing another generation. Parents are teachers, children are students, and the Bible is the textbook. God is indeed the Principal who establishes the teaching guidelines. The questions are, What are we teaching? and How effective is the program we are using?

Weapons or Witnesses

The Bible teaches us that children are arrows in the quiver of their Father (Ps. 17:4). It further commands us to not provoke our children to wrath (Eph. 6:4). For many years, I did not understand the theories behind these scriptures. Finally, it dawned on me that arrows are weapons. Therefore, our children, if they are arrows, can either become a weapon or a witness. Understanding the attributes of how arrows work can assist us in understanding how God intended for parents to rear children.

First of all, arrows must be directed. I have three children. One of them, Jazmyn, has an unusual way with children. Kimberly excels academically, especially in math. My son, James, enjoys people and has the gift of influence on his life. As their parents, my wife, Valerie, and I are charged and called by God to direct and to aim them. While I believe everyone should be able to make their own decisions, the Bible declares that God knows the plans He has for us. In fact, our destiny was declared before we were formed in our mother's womb. Kimberly has been directed to major in accounting. Jazmyn will go to college and major in early childhood education. My son, James, is enrolled at Virginia Union in seminary. We directed or aimed them based upon what we saw in them.

Parents are always asking their children what they want to be when they grow up. Parents should really be observing their children to see the destiny that God has gifted them with and then aim them in the direction of their destiny. Arrows are aimed at targets. Parents should be helping their children establish goals that push them toward a target—their destiny.

Next, arrows are released. Once a target is established, the archer, or the parents in this case, must stretch the bow in order to release the arrow. The principle behind this is the principle of stretching. An arrow's potential traveling distance is based upon how far the bow is stretched. In other words, an arrow can only go as far as the bow is stretched. We must stretch children. Our children were not allowed to choose their own classes in high school. We chose classes for them based upon the target. However, if one of our children had expressed a desire to do a particular thing, if their schedule permitted, we would allow them the latitude to explore the topic. For example, Jazmyn expressed a desire to become a lawyer. We enrolled her in a business law class. She quickly learned (what we already knew) that she hated reading and that she was not interested in that subject matter. Kimberly was inquisitive as well. She had expressed a desire to be a fashion designer. She, too, was given the latitude to take a fashion design class. She thought the class would be simply about drawing designs. However, she quickly found out that she would have to learn all about the different fabrics, cuts, and other parts of fashion design, about which she had no desire.

Even their summer jobs were based upon the target. Jazmyn works for the academy of our church. Kimberly works for the ministry by doing simple accounting transactions. James works in the family life center. They are being developed and stretched. Jazmyn could be called upon to run the academy in the future, and Kimberly could be the executive pastor. My son leads the security ministry, supervises the family life center, and very often offers impromptu counseling to teens and young adults because his gift of influence impacts the decisions that people make in life. We noticed early on that my son used his basketball connections to win people to the kingdom. They all are being aimed. The targets are clearly pointed out to them.

Finally, arrows require a lot of maintenance. They must be kept sharp and straight. Discipline is the vehicle that should be used to make sure the arrows, our children, are properly equipped and capable of hitting the target with the required force to be successful. When my children were growing up, they did not work for the money they earned but for the experience. They were required to save their pay earned during the summer to buy school clothes. I was required to teach them the value and the respect for money. Money is currency. Currency means that money has power. Therefore, if money is not respected it can be dangerous, because unrespected currency can kill.

Arrows that are not respected and properly aimed become destructive. That is why there are so many children participating in crime-related activities. They are weapons that have not been properly stewarded and aimed.

Mo Money, Mo Money, Mo Money

A few months ago, I was blessed to take my daughter to college for the first time. As I watched children from all over America enroll in school, one thing broke my heart. I watched young people with hundred-dollar sneakers on, hundred-dollar jeans, gold fronts in their mouths, and gold chains around their necks standing in the financial aid line. I wanted to ask their parents what they had been doing for eighteen years. Parents have failed to teach their children how to handle money properly. I believe several things have contributed to this failure.

 Parents have failed to teach their children how to handle money properly.

Have you ever stopped to really think about what we teach our children when we give them an allowance? An allowance should be used for one of two reasons: to teach them money management or to teach them not to expect something for nothing. Please hear me out. The principle of allowance is not bad, but the process that we use might be bad. Please remember, we are training a generation to live productively in society. In society, no one is going to get an "allowance," money for doing nothing. They will get paid for doing work. If you use an allowance to teach your children that money is tied to work, then connect their allowance to household chores. Let it be their compensation, or pay, for doing their job. Children have always had jobs and chores to do in the home. Daily jobs such as washing the dishes and taking out the trash are routine in most households. Just as in the real world, if you do not work, you do not get paid. If you work a partial week, you get paid partial salary. I believe allowances used in this manner should be directly connected to work assignments and paid based upon the level of assignments completed. If the assignments are completed two out of five days, then allowance should be based on that same ratio.

Allowance is the opportunity to teach work ethics. In our home, an allowance was used to teach money management. Our children had daily chores, as described earlier; however, it is our belief that children are a part of the family unit and should be taught that daily chores are assigned to everyone in the household to help the household function. As such, there is no allowance associated with fulfilling your part of the family chores. Everyone has to pitch in and help the household to be maintained. There were definitely consequences to chores not being completed; however, the discipline was not necessarily tied to their allowance. In our home, the allowance amount established was determined and adjusted based upon several factors: their age (as they got older, they required a higher allowance), weekly lunch money, their gas, hanging out money, school activity dues, and tithes, among other examples. Once our children reached middle school, their allowance money was provided every Friday. They were required to manage their money properly for the week to take care of all the expenditures we had told them were included in their allowance amount. They could spend it all at the mall on Saturday, but there would be no additional money until the next Friday. They would have to fix their lunch or make other arrangements if they spent their lunch money at the movies. This accomplished several things. First, it taught them money management. It also taught them responsibility. Finally, it taught them to work and to appreciate what they had.

You will find that children make totally different decisions when spending their "own" money. We found that our children will visit the sales rack first when spending their money, rather than heading directly for the designer items when we were making the purchases. It is more difficult to spend money you have worked for on items you know you really do not need and when you know there is no more money coming. Parents, whatever reasons you use for giving an allowance, you must be consistent and stick by the rules you establish in order for the process to work. Your children will test you to see if they can get more. You must resist. Their future employer will not advance them more money. You do not want them constantly coming back to you in the future asking you for a loan. There are too many adults now who never learned the lesson, "There is no more when you have spent it all." That is why so many adults are in credit card debt. When the money is gone, they simply charge it. Your son or daughter will not die from starvation if he or she misses a lunch or two because they spent their lunch money. They will learn to either be hungry, pack that lunch, or budget their money wisely. Isn't this what you are trying to teach them early in life?

My wife has always been very conscious of teaching our children how to handle and manage money. Very early, she opened saving accounts for all of our children. They are required to pay their tithes and to save established amounts of their money. In fact, our children have been trained to live on 70 percent of their income. Ten percent belongs to God. Ten percent should be saved, and ten percent should be used to change the lives of those around you in the community and the world. My father-in-law also reinforced our teaching. On birthdays and at Christmas, he rarely would give toys. He would always give them savings bonds. This forced them to understand the power of saving, as well as provided a great investment for their futures. Our children did not appreciate them when they were young; however, now that they are grown and have a substantial savings, they are delighted. Our son was able to have money to use as a down payment for a condo.

We teach our children daily through our examples how to handle money. When they observe us driving a ninety thousand dollar car but see us give five dollars in the church offering, we are teaching. Our children learn by observing us. We teach our children to become givers by allowing them to observe a spirit of giving in us. At Christmas, our children were shown how to be givers by observing us give to others. As our children got older, we also allowed them to participate in the processes of purchasing our homes and our vehicles by going with us to the closing or the attorney's office and listening and observing. We wanted them informed and educated. I am proud of the fact that at the age of twenty-three, my son is buying his first home.

On Christmas, I would require our children to give to those in the community. We would wake up early Christmas day and drive to nearby homes. We left gifts on the porches but never identified ourselves. My wife and I have worked diligently to teach our children theories and theology about money: how to spend, how to save, and how to give.

Discipline

The word *discipline* comes from the root word *disciple*. A disciple is a follower or learner. Our children are, indeed, our disciples. They follow us and learn from us. In fact, they are our disciples whether we desire them to be or not. We do not have a choice in being the example for them. They follow us in all things. They observe and duplicate the behavior that we display. Discipline, then, should be the instrument we use to teach and train their behavior. Not long ago, I was talking with a local juvenile judge in our area, and he shared something critically important with me. He shared that how we discipline our children is totally contrary to the process employed by society. We, in fact, train them to expect the same treatment from the judge that they receive at home. This is not healthy. Based upon the education on discipline that the judge gave me, I have learned that there are some things we can do to provide our children with the best possible opportunity for success. When we discipline our children, it should include four areas: consideration, calculation, consistency, and completion. Let's explore these areas further.

Emotional times are the worst moments for discipline. A good night's sleep, a moment of reflection, and a deep breath can make the time of discipline much more effective.

When we are about to discipline our children, there are several considerations that need to be observed. First, every child is different. What works for one child may not work for another child. This must be considered. Spanking may work with one child, while taking away the right to watch television may work with another child. Another consideration is the severity of the inappropriate behavior. Many times we do not consider the fact that the restriction should be related and equal to the incident. We can establish a process of restriction that is too severe or not severe enough to meet the need of behavior adjustment when we operate out of our emotions. Finally, we must consider if we are in the right frame of mind to determine how to handle the behavior of the child. Emotional times are the worst moments for discipline. A good night's sleep, a moment of reflection, and a deep breath can make the time of discipline much more effective.

After we have had time to properly receive information and have considered all of the discipline options, we are ready to move to stage two, which is calculation. Calculation involves managing the time of discipline. Many times parents will give a plan of discipline that they cannot enforce or monitor. Why establish boundaries that cannot be carried out properly? When we discipline our children, we should be prepared to adjust our schedule or make any other needed changes in order to properly manage the discipline plan. You cannot manage television restriction if you are not at home (unless you lock the cable box with a code). Young people are very intelligent. They are already thinking about ways of escape before we are passing the sentence. We must calculate the restriction. Restriction must be monitored in order to remain effective.

Another need for calculation is based upon the frequency and severity of the negative activity or behavior. Is this the first time the behavior has been discovered? Is this a first offence? How did the child respond during the discovery of the behavior? How much planning had to go into the behavior? Before the sentence is passed, calculation must take place.

Stage three of any discipline plan should include consistency. The establishing of a consistent plan of discipline prevents us from having to deal with any unexpected surprises. When we establish consistent boundaries, our children begin to discipline themselves. When I speak about consistency, I mean responding to the same behavior at all times from all children. For instance, we cannot allow our children to break curfew sometimes. Consequences must be provided anytime the curfew is broken. When we make exceptions, we confuse young people. The system in which they live is clear on the behavior that is not accepted. Inconsistent discipline causes young people to expect to get away with unacceptable behavior at certain times. Therefore, we must be consistent. Right is right and wrong is wrong all the time.

Finally, any successful discipline plan must be completed. One of the areas in which parents fail the most is in plan completion. If the restriction is for a week, then a week should be completed. Remember the judge I talked about earlier? He shared how this is perhaps the greatest place of detriment to our children. Most children know that if they can adjust their behavior for a couple of days, then their restriction will be ended based upon good behavior. Many times parents use the language, "The next time you do it…" This actually teaches young people to expect multiple chances to display unacceptable behavior before suffering any consequences. Good, positive reinforcement is based upon clearly expressing what will happen and then doing what was said. If the restriction is a week of no television, then one full week it must be. Remember, we are teaching our children.

In the larger system of our courts, the judge will have to do what he says, and they will have to comply with what the judge says. As parents, we should desire to equip our children to succeed. A part of this teaching is making sure that they understand how the larger system operates. We must reinforce that understanding, remain consistent with our discipline plan, and insist that the plan be completed. It takes time and effort, but the Bible declares that a child left to himself will bring his mother shame. When we invest the time and energy required to develop discipline plans and operate within the confines of the plans, our children will mature and develop into the productive citizens we desire them to be and that God deserves.

Chapter 17

Who's the Banker?

EARLIER, I SHARED HOW immature I was when I got married. Not only was I immature, but I thought with perspectives that were a problem for our marriage. One of the perspectives was relative to who should handle the money. First, let me say that I was reared by a mother to whom I gave my paycheck without question. I knew that she needed to pay bills, but she was also a gambler. This caused me to become very angry and very protective of who had access to my money. When I got married, I did not really want my wife to control the money as a result of my financial baggage. I did not trust anyone, and as I described earlier, I was committed to making sure that no one told me what I could or could not do with my money.

My wife was a practicing Certified Public Accountant (CPA) who was taking care of financial matters for corporations, yet I would not allow her to handle the household finances. She was working two jobs and bringing home more money than I was, but I wanted to handle the money. On top of that, my wife is more disciplined than I am and has always been committed to saving. I am a spender, spender, spender!

We discussed handling the money. I was adamant that I would handle the money. All of my financial baggage finally caused us to be overdrawn at the bank and behind on most of our bills. We were not behind because we did not have sufficient resources to meet our obligations. We were behind because the person handling the finances was not the most qualified. I insisted on handling the finances, but I was not good at it. By the time I turned the finances over to my wife, we were drastically over-drawn and in financial trouble. We had several hundred dollars in past-due bank fees, and creditors were calling the house daily.

The first question any couple has to answer is, Who will be the banker? The banker is not decided based on gender but based on qualification. In every marriage, there is someone who handles the finances better than the other person. One person must be designated to handle the financial responsibilities of the home. It does not make them smarter; it does not make them the boss; it simply makes them responsible. In fact, all respon-sibilities should be assigned. I cut the grass better than my wife, so I cut the grass. But cutting the grass is not "a man's job;" it belongs to the person who does it the best.

Not only should we decide who will handle the finan-cial responsibilities, but we must also decide how they will be handled. Will we have separate accounts or joint accounts? Often I am asked, "Which process is the best?" The answer is whatever works best in your household. Because some people have jobs that provide sporadic income and not a predetermined salary, sometimes two accounts are better. However, I usually try to get couples to understand that they are one and should have one household account. My experience has shown that having one corporate, household account into which both spouses deposit their income works best. This general account should contain the bulk of the couple's money and should be used to pay the household bills. It should be a joint account in the name of both spouses. Each spouse can have a separate account for their personal satisfaction and spending, but those accounts should be secondary to the main account. The income for these secondary accounts should be based on an agreed upon "allowance" for per diem expenses that both husband and wife receive weekly, bi-weekly, or monthly. Even these secondary accounts should be accessible by the spouse for legal reasons and the building of trust. Secret accounts, or accounts that are not fully accessible by both spouses, only create an atmosphere that causes a lack of trust. When we keep secrets, we impact truth. Complete financial disclosure is important. If you do not feel comfortable sharing financial information with your spouse, then there are deeper concerns that must be dealt with.

As with anything, there are always special circumstances that can be the exception to the rule. When a spouse has proven to have difficulty with access to finances because of things like spending addictions or substance abuse, systems might need to be put into place in order to prevent behavior that is detrimental to the family's financial stability. Every couple must evaluate its personal financial program and make decisions as a couple that put them in position for the greatest potential financial success.

 Goals should be attainable but also should require some stretching.

Goal Setting

One of the areas that many couples fall short in is developing financial goals. A couple should sit down annually and develop financial goals. How much do we desire to save during the year? How much do we desire to give during the year? How much are we going to spend on other goals, like vacations? Goals should be attainable but also should require some stretching. Many times we make our goals unrealistic. Goals should be based upon our mutual agreement and desires. We have a limited amount of resources in which to fund these goals, so goals may need to be prioritized.

Goals also accomplish at least two other things. First, they allow us to have a reason to say no that is not subjective. We can handle the answer no when there is tangible evidence supporting the reason for the answer. It prevents the answer "no" from appearing to be personal and unfair. If something does not fit with the goals, then we should not do it. Secondly, goals allow us to build motivation for our commitment. It is hard to sacrifice when we never see any improvement and never feel the excitement of victory or success. When we set and reach goals, it makes the sacrifice worthwhile. Achieving goals feeds our emotions and provides gratification. In short, we feel better when we see progress. Financial goal-setting is really about changing our financial behavior and the way in which we think about money.

The Family Budget

I have found that many people really do not know where the money goes. We spend a great amount of money that we do not track. The daily cup of coffee, the morning donut, stopping at the grocery store daily, and fast food lunches are drains on any family's finances. A budget can be a vehicle that not only controls spending but tells us where we spend. Every family needs a budget, but a budget is only as good as our commitment to live by the budget. Many families create a budget, but they do not make it detailed enough. The budget should include every single place where every cent might leave the household: bills, allowances, recreation, savings, and contingency funds are areas of vital importance when creating a budget.

Everyone in the family should be aware of the budget. The budget should guide all spending decisions. Even big-ticket items such as car purchases should be included in the budget. For instance, my wife has decided we will never have a budget without a car allowance because I like buying cars. Once again, even the most detailed items should also be in the budget. Everything from haircuts, hair salon treatments, dinner, and Christmas spending should be included in the budget. The more detailed and comprehensive the budget, the higher the likelihood of controlled spending. The budget should reflect established financial goals, such as: savings, investments, and college funds. Budgets that are developed (or reviewed) annually establish benchmarks for handling pay raises as well. Many people increase their spending when they receive a raise. A raise is pure surplus. Money that we did not have earlier can be saved or rerouted into more productive areas for our financial future.

Establish Boundaries

The budget should work hand-in-hand with our financial boundaries. Financial boundaries are really based upon our financial theories. Husbands and wives must establish spending principles and financial parameters. For instance, I think buying a new car is a terrible investment, so we have established a boundary about car purchases. New cars depreciate greatly the moment you drive them off the lot, so we only buy late-model used cars. They maintain better value and you pass the depreciation on to someone else. You can also purchase an extended warranty on these types of cars that give you better service than a new car warranty does. Another financial boundary that we live by is credit card debt. We do not have extended credit card debt. We use credit cards only for emergencies. We pay them off monthly. Neither of us can have a credit card that the other spouse is not aware of. All credit cards must be accessible to both of us. Any and all big-ticket purchases are decided upon by both spouses. These boundaries prevent us from corrupting our financial plans and give structure and definition to our financial decisions. We also have established boundaries about what type of loans and interest rates are acceptable for our family. We have even included decisions about purchasing groceries, buying lunch, and spending money for college in our budget. We decided that our children would not be allowed to get loans for college unless they were attempting to go to medical school or law school or some career field that generates sufficient income to justify the amount of student loans. For example, it does not make sense (to us) to borrow one hundred thousand dollars to go to a particular school to become a teacher. Nothing is wrong with being a teacher; however, teachers' salaries are fixed. Therefore, a person graduating from a less expensive school will make the same as the person with one hundred thousand dollars in loans. The child graduating with the one hundred thousand dollars in student loans starts life off farther behind financially than the same child who has no student loans. The child heavily laden with the student loan debt far too often finds himself/herself facing bankruptcy, credit card debt, or a financially scrapped life that could have been avoided, had they been given better counsel before making the decision to take out the student loans.

Boundaries do not have to be written, but they must be clearly defined and understood by both husband and wife. Writing them only makes them clearer and takes away any excuses. Financial boundaries establish a financial order for the family, while allowing every couple to have a set strategy about their decision making and money management. A budget, boundaries, and a banker take the teeth out of many arguments. We are a product of the decisions we make. Creating an atmosphere that enables us to make better decisions will release and liberate our financial stress. When the family is doing well financially, the level of harmony and peace is positively affected and the relationship between husband and wife is blessed beyond measure.

Handling Debt

Many marital relationships are stressed because we have not properly managed our spending. There are some rules of thumb that can help alleviate a great deal of the stress that comes from bad money management. First of all, we must recognize the problem and identify the root cause of our financial stress. In the case of my marriage, our problem was that I was a binge spender and not good at managing the household spending. To correct this, we made several decisions. I gave up all of my credit cards and bank cards. As hard as that was to do, it was necessary for the financial health of my family. I also turned the handling of the finances over to my wife. These changes have been extremely beneficial to placing our family in a financially healthy position. We made a conscious decision that we would have no less than six months of household living expenses in our savings at all times. This gave us the ability to ride out some bad times. I call this the six-month rule. While this does take discipline, it will prove to be well worth the discipline, should you ever hit a bump in your financial future.

When planning to get a handle on debt, the discipline to destroy credit cards is vital. While we should be committed to establishing credit, having too many credit cards can be a problem. Credit cards that are versatile and useable at many places are best because they prevent us from needing multiple credit cards. The interest rate should always be monitored, and a fixed rate is more desirable. Credit cards that require the balance to be paid monthly are preferred because they allow credit to be established, while also forcing the individuals to be disciplined in their spending.

Credit cards should not be a substitute for capital but should mainly be used for emergency purchases. When attempting to pay off credit cards, you should begin by paying off the card with the highest interest rate. Also, credit cards should be attacked one at a time. Many times, you can also call the credit card company and negotiate your payoff. I have found that a call to the credit card company is the best way to handle payments that are late. To do nothing is a bad decision. Call and honestly share your situation. The credit card company will usually appreciate the call. The call will begin a process of repayment, and most companies are committed to working with the debtor.

Any plan is only as good as your personal discipline. Cut the card up or give it to someone who can hold it for you until you really need it. Watch your spending trends and patterns. Because we do not all have the same level of income, many times we have to watch with whom we shop. Peer pressure can influence you to spend beyond your capability. One of our relatives is in the NFL. Although he makes great money, as the NFL goes, he cannot compete in spending with many of the young men in the league who were first- and second-round draft picks. He has to be sensitive to whom he hangs out with, because not everyone is making the same amount of money.

 When we steward our finances properly, we position ourselves to bless the kingdom and receive more opportunity from God.

Deciding to establish financial goals, set financial boundaries, and commit to good stewardship can lead to the opportunity to develop a strong financial foundation. This foundation can create an atmosphere in marriage that will enable us to live within our means. Remember, money is not evil; but the *love* of money is the root of all evil (1 Tim. 6:10). When we steward our finances properly, we position ourselves to bless the kingdom and receive more opportunity from God. We must display behavior that proves we can be trusted with more. Money is simply a vehicle to support the kingdom. Our plans, decisions, and stewardship should prove that we can be trusted and have a clear understanding of how to manage money. It is never too late to begin to change our attitudes and retrain our thinking. Debt is not bad, but unmanaged debt can be.

Afterword

WE HAVE COME A long way together. We have discussed almost every area of marriage. While I did not go as deep as we could in every area, I have attempted to challenge your thinking, perspectives, and ideologies. Perhaps, with the power of the Almighty, your thinking has been changed in areas such as parenting, sexuality, finances, communication, and expectations. We live in a society where divorce rates are constantly rising, and currently they are above fifty percent. That means that for every one hundred people that read this book, fifty of them will get a divorce. That figure is unacceptable. This book has not been an attempt to argue marriage perspectives but to save marriages by building healthier, stronger marriages. It was not my desire to judge anyone but rather to encourage everyone who reads this book to take a good, hard look at themselves. I still believe in rainbows. I still believe in miracles. And I still believe in marriage. I pray that just as God did a work and performed a miracle in my marriage, miracles will take place in the lives of readers. I pray that somewhere a husband is warming a towel for his wife, having it ready when she gets out of the shower. I pray that a wife is not upset with her husband for not responding because she now better understands that he needs time in the cave. I pray that even at this time, Satan is being destroyed because a warring, seeing, wife is pointing him out to her warrior husband.

This represents the best that I have. I have offered my best and pray that God will take it, use it, add to it, and anoint it. One by one, our marriages will be changed. As God heals and empowers each of our marital relationships, we must become marriage evangelists. Please announce to others what the power of God can do if we are open to His Spirit and voice. Pass on what you have learned. It all begins with two small words—"I do."

Notes

Chapter 4—Understanding Your Spouse

1. Emily Marlin, *Genograms* (Chicago: Contemporary Books, 1989), 12.

2. Ibid.

3. Ibid.

4. Ibid.

About the Author

KIM W. BROWN IS the senior pastor of Mount Lebanon Baptist Church in Chesapeake, Virginia, and Elizabeth City, North Carolina, and presides over Kingdom Keepers Fellowship of Pastors, an organization serving Christian Leaders and pastors across America. He is a graduate of Norfolk State University, and holds both an M.Div, and D.Min from Virginia Union University, in Richmond, Virginia. His out-of-the-box approach to ministry has enabled the ministry to grow from 75 to over 4,000 partners, with three ministry campuses in two states. He is a gifted preacher and builder of people, with a heart to serve the community. He currently serves as the Chair of the Board for the Chesapeake Regional Medical Center in Chesapeake, Virginia. He resides in Virginia with his wife and Executive Pastor, Valerie. They have three children, James, Kimberly, and Jazmyn.

To Contact the Author

For more information visit www.
themountleads.org.